ROLLS-ROYCE

AT DERBY

This scene at Nightingale Road could have been during the 1930s but in fact is much later, around 1950. The vehicle is a Phantom II that has been converted to a fire tender. Working at Nightingale Road during the 1920s and 1930s meant that one had to be on duty before 7.55am. The first of two hooters, which were known as 'bulls', sounded at 7.50am with the second sounding five minutes later, after which the gates closed. Anyone arriving late was locked out until lunchtime and docked half a day's pay. (Courtesy Rolls-Royce & Bentley Motor Cars)

ROLLS-ROYCE AT DERBY

MALCOLM BOBBITT

DB
PUBLISHING

First published in Great Britain byThe Breedon Books Publishing Company
Limited Breedon House, 44 Friar Gate, Derby, DE1 1DA. 1999

This paperback edition published in Great Britain in 2015 by DB Publishing, an imprint of
JMD Media Ltd

ISBN 978-1-78091-497-8

Printed and bound in the UK by Copytech (UK) Ltd Peterborough

CONTENTS

ACKNOWLEDGEMENTS

This book would not have been possible without the help of the following people who have done much in the way of contributing information and photographs. In particular I would like to thank Peter Baines of the Rolls-Royce Enthusiasts' Club, and Philip Hall, curator of the Sir Henry Royce Memorial Foundation. Both have allowed me access to archives and photographic collections. Richard Haigh of the Rolls-Royce Heritage Trust has provided some essential information, and Rolls-Royce and Bentley Motor Cars have afforded me access to photographic collections for which I am very grateful. My thanks to Bernard King who has supplied helpful advice on a number of issues, and to Oliver Suffield who has given me the benefit of his experience concerning those Bentley motor cars that were built at Derby and which have become known as Derby Bentleys. Other Bentley material is courtesy of Douglas Trotter and Rolf Knoery.

I am indebted to the library staff at the National Motor Museum at Beaulieu, and the efforts of Jonathan Day in particular; to David Fletcher at the Tank Museum at Bovington, and to Christine Gregory at the RAF Museum, Hendon. There has been much painstaking research regarding events in Derby, and therefore the assistance given by Derby Libraries staff and the team at the *Derby Evening Telegraph* is gratefully acknowledged.

Thanks, too, to Martin Bourne, Andrew Minney and Richard Mann, all of whom have made the task of writing this book less awesome. Had it not been for Rupert Harding and the publishing team at Breedon, this book would certainly not have materialised. Finally my gratitude is extended to my wife Jean for her usual tolerance and forbearance during months of research and foraging among archive material.

Malcolm Bobbitt, Cumbria, 2002

INTRODUCTION

ROLLS-ROYCE has been synonymous with Derby for well over 90 years, the factory having been opened on 9 July 1908 at Nightingale Road on land that had once formed the Osmaston estate. The history of Rolls-Royce extends to even earlier times when, before his association with C.S. Rolls, Henry Royce was building Royce cars at Cooke Street in Manchester in 1904, having already established himself as a manufacturer of electrical equipment.

The reason for moving from Manchester was that the premises in Cooke Street had become too small for the expanding company, and relocating to a greenfield site offered an opportunity to develop the business of building luxury motor cars. Derby could well not have been the chosen site for Rolls-Royce as the company was considering various other locations, including Leicester and Nottingham. That Derby was chosen has added to the city's fortunes.

Today Rolls-Royce at Derby is recognised for its aero-engine business, which is the finest in the world and the leader in aviation technology. The Rolls-Royce trademark, the R-R monogram, is not only a symbol of success, but also the pride of the British nation and a mark of quality and expertise. The diversity of the company has allowed its products to be used in every aspect of industry, from shipping to railways, oil exploration and beyond.

Although motor cars have not been produced at Nightingale Road since 1939, motor vehicles bearing the famous monogram nevertheless remain much associated with Derby. Models such as the Silver Ghost were built at the factory for customers for whom nothing less than a Rolls-Royce would suffice. The company's clientele were the most discerning of motorists and included royalty and heads of state. Cars were produced until the outbreak of war in 1939, and although the factory had concentrated on the war effort between 1914 and 1919, it nevertheless produced armoured cars based on the Silver Ghost chassis during that period. Motor cars built after the Silver Ghost era were eagerly received, and today the 20hp and the 20/25, 25/30hp and Phantom models are not only sought after by loyal Rolls-Royce enthusiasts, but also continue to provide sterling service.

The fortunes of Rolls-Royce were built on people, and this remains true to this day. Without the efforts, often beyond the call of duty, of those connected with the company, Rolls-Royce would probably not now be at the leading edge of technology. The company was established on strong fundamental principles. 'Whatever is rightly done, however humble, is noble', was Royce's edict.

'The fortunes of Rolls-Royce were built on people...'

'Whatever is rightly done, however humble, is noble.'
H. Royce

During the late 1920s Rolls-Royce's experimental department was evaluating a series of three Sports Phantoms, one of which (chassis 16EX) is depicted outside the main entrance to the company's offices at Nightingale Road, Derby. Originally carrying the registration number CH 7234, the car has Barker coachwork finished in Curzon Blue with polished aluminium and was pictured after it had been released from the experimental department and made ready for sale. The registration number was changed to GK12. In January 1929 the vehicle was sold to Captain J.F.C. Kruse, who sold it a year later to A.S. Fuller of London. This photograph was taken some time after 1931, as shown by the Bentley Motors (1931) Limited plaque on the right-hand side of the office entrance and above the door. (Courtesy Rolls-Royce & Bentley Motor Cars Ltd)

Throughout its tenure in Derby Rolls-Royce has provided employment for thousands of people. Some 400 were employed at Nightingale Road when the factory opened. That number doubled within four years, and the ranks had swollen to 4,000 by the mid-1920s. During World War Two the extended workforce toiled relentlessly to provide for the war effort.

Rolls, too, was a pioneer, both as a motorist and as an aviator. Together Rolls and Royce made an ideal partnership, although they came from opposite ends of the class spectrum. Socially they may have been distant, but there was a common link between them: both demanded only the very best.

According to Rolls-Royce lore, the hyphen linking Rolls and Royce was personified by Claude Johnson, another of motoring's pioneers. More often than not Johnson was the driving force at Rolls-Royce, for he understood the two partners completely, and they both had total trust in him. When Rolls was tragically killed in a flying accident in 1910 it was Johnson who supported Royce, and when Henry Royce experienced chronic illness it was Johnson who took over the running of the company. The fact that Claude Johnson was able to assume the company mantle is testament to the fact that the workforce at Nightingale Road was loyal.

Rolls-Royce began building aero-engines in 1914, and had it not been for the success of the Eagle, the company's very first aero-engine, it is doubtful whether Britain would have been as successful as she was during World War One. It was the Eagle that powered Alcock and Brown's pioneering trans-Atlantic flight in their Vickers Vimy in 1919, and the same engine type was responsible for the first flight from England to Australia during the same year.

Commentators on British history often refer to Rolls-Royce as having provided the strength to win the Battle of Britain in World War Two. If they mean that Rolls-Royce Merlin and Griffon engines powered Spitfires, Hurricanes and other aircraft in battle, then that is certainly the case.

After World War Two motor car production resumed not at Derby but at Crewe, at the company's shadow factory, which itself had contributed majestically to the war effort. It was at Derby, however, that the ground was laid for a new era in aviation, the jet engine. Had it not been for Ernest Hives, who had taken over as general manager of Rolls-Royce after Sir Henry Royce's death in 1933, the success of Frank Whittle's invention might never have been fully realised. Hives was very much of the Rolls-Royce tradition, and it was through his efforts that Derby cultivated aero-engineering, to the extent that it is now the world leader.

Throughout the 90 years or so that it has been based in Derby, Rolls-Royce has experienced highs and lows: highs when developing new techniques and winning orders for the company, Derby and Britain, and lows when economic gloom produces downturns in business.

During the last 30 years or so there have been two catastrophic events within Rolls-Royce. In 1971 development of the RB211 aero-engine created huge financial problems for the company, and the date of 4 February 1971 is engraved on the minds of everyone who was associated with Rolls-Royce at the time.

Then, in 2001, the events that followed terrorist attacks in America on 11 September were responsible for a dramatic collapse in the aviation business. As this introduction is being written, the full effects of the measures taken by Rolls-Royce to tackle overheads and realign cost and capacity with demand have yet to be appreciated. However, Rolls-Royce has survived previous calamities, and it will do so again.

Malcolm Bobbitt, Cumbria, 2002.

CHAPTER ONE

PIONEERING DAYS

THE R-R MONOGRAM is among the most respected trademarks in the world. Airline passengers take comfort from knowing that the intertwined 'Rs' adorning engine casings on modern jets are the symbol of unsurpassed engineering excellence. Motorists, too, recognise the monogram as exemplifying attention to detail on arguably the most prestigious of motor vehicles.

Rolls-Royce is synonymous with Derby, the Nightingale Road factory having been officially opened on 9 July 1908. Many alterations have been made to the factory over the years, and today it is somewhat larger than when first built. Nevertheless, the original buildings remain, and are integral to the works' daily operations. Although this book is devoted to Derby, it would be an omission not to mention the Crewe works, which were built in the second half of the 1930s as a shadow factory to provide aero-engines to replenish Britain's severely depleted military arsenal. After World War Two motor car production was transferred from Derby to Crewe in order that the Nightingale Road premises might expand and extend its aero-engine expertise, for which it was rightly recognised. During the aftermath of war Rolls-Royce spearheaded a rapidly developing avionics industry, and today the company is a world leader.

The Derby factory has not always been recognised as the nucleus of aero-engine technology. When it opened, Nightingale Road was for the building of motor cars, and after Rolls-Royce incorporated Bentley Motors in 1931, which until then had been based at Cricklewood in north London, Derby became the new home of that eminent marque. There was always, nevertheless, a likelihood that Derby would become associated with the aviation industry. The Hon. C.S. Rolls, co-founder of Rolls-Royce

Motor Cars and Rolls-Royce Limited, was, before he was tragically killed in a flying accident, totally committed to all aspects of aeronautics, and it would only have been a matter of time before the assembly lines were busy producing avionic components. It was during World War One that Derby officially became involved with aero-engine manufacturing, and from then on until the onset of World War Two the chassis and aero-engine divisions worked in close harmony.

Manchester Origins

Rolls-Royce at Derby owes its origins to the great manufacturing city of Manchester, where Henry Royce began building motors cars in 1904. Like so many of his contemporaries, Royce had taken an interest in the development of motor cars, the fledgling British motor industry having been largely influenced by the French and Germans. Royce's first experience of a motorised vehicle was with a De Dion quadricycle, which he was persuaded to acquire by his doctor, who suggested it as an alternative activity to relentless hard work.

The therapy which the De Dion was supposed to have provided did not fully materialise, and ultimately Royce collapsed. Unable to work, Royce and his wife Minnie took a voyage to Cape Town to visit relatives. On his return to England, the revitalised Royce decided to part with the De Dion and search for a vehicle of greater substance.

In time Royce became interested in and bought a French Decauville, a much more sophisticated machine and one that had connections with some of the most highly regarded French motor cars. There have been some interesting theories surrounding Royce's purchase. Some historians believe that he questioned the car's reliability, and thus dismantled the machine to rebuild it to his own exacting standards. Others argue more positively that Royce bought what he considered to be one of the best cars of the time, and took it pieces to establish exactly how it operated. In the early 1900s, to quote the late John Bolster, 'French cars were quite simply recognised as the best.'

Smitten by the motor car and the independence it afforded, Royce acknowledged that the 'horseless carriage' would revolutionise personal transportation. His experience with the Decauville, and the huge amount of interest the Thousand Miles Motor Vehicle Trial of 1900 had created, provoked Royce to build his own prototype car in the spring of 1903. Having a sound business instinct, Royce undertook the dismantling of the Decauville very carefully, and he established at the Cooke Street premises a car drawing office with two personnel, along with three works' apprentices. This alone illustrates that the building of the prototype motor car was not just to satisfy a mere curiosity. Two further prototypes were planned, which shows that Royce had given serious thought to entering car production.

It was a year before the first Royce motor car took to the road. Again there is some conjecture about the event: for a long time the date of the prototype run was believed to have been 31 March, when in fact it was Good Friday, 1 April. There is evidence that as the engine of the motor car fired into action, and the vehicle was driven out of the works followed by the rebuilt Decauville, the atmosphere in Cooke Street resembled a carnival. Royce employees, it is said, demonstrated their enthusiasm by banging anything that made a noise, the racket being audible in the surrounding streets. The uproar probably did not

Frederick Henry Royce was born in 1863, the son of a miller, at Alwalton near Peterborough. His father died when Henry was nine and afterwards he was brought up by his mother and aunt. To supplement the family income the young Henry had to sell newspapers, and at the age of 12, by which time he had no more than three years of schooling, he began work as a telegraph boy before beginning an apprenticeship with the Great Northern Railway. Despite Royce not completing his apprenticeship owing to financial hardship, he nevertheless gained much experience which stood him in good stead when he established his own electrical and crane-making business. Later he diversified into motor cars and aero-engine manufacturing. Years of toil resulted in Royce experiencing chronic illness at a relatively early age. Having designed and developed the Derby factory, which opened on 9 July 1908, Royce spent very little time there, and instead worked in the kinder climates of the south of France and the south coast of England. Royce died in 1933. (Courtesy Rolls-Royce & Bentley Motor Cars Ltd)

Before Rolls and Royce formed their partnership, C.S. Rolls had established a business selling and repairing motor cars at Lillie Hall, Fulham. This photograph dates from around 1905 and a number of Rolls-Royce machines can be seen. In addition to Rolls-Royce, C.S. Rolls & Co. were agents for Mors, Minerva, Panhard and Peugeot, among others. Lillie Hall closed at the end of 1970 when Rover Hire took over the premises, and it was demolished in 1991. (Courtesy Rolls-Royce & Bentley Motor Cars Ltd)

impress Royce, but on this occasion he no doubt turned a deaf ear. The cars were driven to Knutsford and back, a distance of some 15 miles, and were undoubtedly greeted with renewed clamour.

That some discord existed between Henry Royce and his business partner Ernest Claremont, with whom he had established his electrical and crane manufacturing firm in 1884, is in little doubt. Claremont did not always share Royce's enthusiasm for motoring, and when he was presented with the second prototype car he found the machine unreliable. Claremont's anxiety resulted in him having a hansom cab follow the car wherever it went, so that when it broke down he was able to continue his journey by more traditional means. The vehicle allocated to Claremont was used to test modifications as directed by Royce, hence its sometimes questionable reliability, although a number of the recorded incidents were nothing more sinister than running out of petrol. It must be said, however, that Royce's motor cars were constructed to the highest of standards, with every part of the machine being meticulously engineered in the interests of quiet and efficient running. It is acknowledged that at the time Royce's cars were among the finest available.

Claremont's sceptism of motor cars may have been caused by an incident that occurred when he was a passenger in a car driven by Royce. The car was

1A and 3 Cooke Street, Hulme, Manchester, where Henry Royce established his electrical manufacturing business in 1884. F.H. Royce & Co. was formed out of the partnership between Royce and Ernest Claremont, with a capital of £70. Records show that Royce's contribution was £20 and Claremont's was £50, and in view of the amounts it is a matter of some curiosity that Claremont's name was not featured. The photograph was taken many years after Royce had moved from the premises, presumably during the 1930s. (Courtesy Sir Henry Royce Memorial Foundation)

allowed to slip against a kerb, and Claremont lost his balance and was thrown out of the car, although he was not injured. Royce, perhaps misunderstanding the situation, remonstrated with Claremont, accusing him of jumping out rather than letting the car right itself. His attitude did little to bolster Claremont's already dim view of motor cars in general.

Two of Royce's apprentices, Eric Platford and Tom Haldenby, were largely responsible for the testing of the prototype 10hp cars. They worked long hours and were involved in virtually every aspect of the cars' development. Platford became chief tester at Rolls-

Royce in later years, and Haldenby established, with Ernest Hives, the Rolls-Royce experimental department. Eric Platford's death in 1938 was premature, but Tom Haldenby retired in 1952 having been appointed as a consultant to Rolls-Royce in respect of the company's plant and buildings.

Eric Platford was given the opportunity to take charge of the second Royce car when it was entered for the Sideslip Trials of April 1904. Ernest Claremont had loaned the car to his friend Henry Edmunds for the duration of the trials, and Ernie Mills, who had joined Royce in 1902, was invited to accompany the duo. Mills's presence must not be undermined in any way; a highly skilled mechanic, he had been instrumental in erecting the first Royce car at Cooke Street.

Henry Edmunds played a key role in the formation of Rolls-Royce. Not only was he a loyal business associate of Ernest Claremont, he also shared a firm friendship with him and his family. Through Claremont, Edmunds knew Henry Royce, and was quick to appreciate his business and engineering acumen. He

Henry Royce's first experience with motorised transport had been with a quadricycle, and it was only a matter of time before he decided to purchase a motor car. His choice was a second-hand French Decauville similar to that depicted here in around 1903. Decauville had a good reputation, which is probably why Royce decided to buy that model. There are several explanations for why Royce ultimately dismantled the car and rebuilt it to his own exacting standards before designing and building his own machine. (Courtesy National Motor Museum)

Having decided to venture into car making, Royce built three prototype machines, the first of which is shown here in chassis form. The 10hp two-cylinder engine incorporated a side exhaust and overhead inlet arrangement, something which Rolls-Royce reverted to after World War Two on their Bentley Mark VI, Silver Dawn and Silver Wraith six-cylinder models. Note that the machine depicted is without a cooling fan which, it is believed, was never fitted to this particular chassis. (Courtesy Rolls-Royce & Bentley Motor Cars Ltd)

Seen here at the back of the Cooke Street Works in the Blake Street stable yard, the first Royce car is being driven by one of the draughtsmen who worked with Royce to transform his ideas into drawings. It will be noted that Royce cars lacked affinity with the more familiar radiator style associated with Rolls-Royce. (Courtesy Sir Henry Royce Memorial Foundation)

also applauded Royce's car building achievements. Edmunds was also a friend of the Hon. Charles S. Rolls, the aviator and pioneer motorist.

Rolls and Edmunds were both exponents of the motor car in its formative years, the two men having privately entered and driven their cars in the Thousand Miles Trial of 1900. The event, held between 23 April and 12 May, was the most adventurous motor trial to date. It was organised by the Automobile Club of Great Britain and Ireland, the object being to increase enthusiasm for the automobile in the United Kingdom.

That the Thousand Miles Trial kick-started the British motor industry is little disputed. The trials were also responsible for Henry Edmunds and C.S. Rolls becoming acquainted, the former driving a Daimler and the latter a Panhard. It is possible that Rolls told Edmunds that he intended establishing a business providing motor cars (which he did in 1902), and that he wished to associate himself with a suitable manufacturer to market a car of his own. When Edmunds learned about Royce's fine automobiles he recommended them to Rolls, sending him drawings, specifications and as much detailed information as was available.

Edmunds's endeavours resulted in the now famous meeting between Henry Royce and C.S. Rolls at the Midland Hotel in Manchester on 4 May 1904. The meeting may have been the culmination of several events, all of which were connected, if somewhat loosely. The aforementioned Thousand Miles Trial was a positive force in the formation of Rolls-Royce. Alfred Harmsworth (later Lord Northcliffe), the Fleet Street newspaper magnate, had entered two cars, a Daimler and a Panhard, and his association with C.S. Rolls was instrumental in cultivating a long relationship with the

company. Claude Johnson, secretary of the Automobile Club, both organised the trial and competed in it. As well as being Rolls's business assistant, Johnson, often later referred to as 'the hyphen in Rolls-Royce', became the company's first managing director.

It could be said that Rolls and Royce were from two quite different levels of society. Rolls, the son of Lord and Lady Llangattock, was born into the aristocracy in 1877. He attended Eton and afterwards Cambridge University, from where he graduated in June 1898 with a degree in Mechanism and Applied Science. Rolls was the first Cambridge undergraduate to own a motor car, and he competed in every motoring event he could.

In 1899 Rolls had established a workshop at South Lodge, Kensington, the family home. Neither an inventor nor designer, Rolls nonetheless had a deep-seated understanding of engineering, something which stood him in good stead in both motoring and aviation. In 1902 he acquired premises at Lillie Hall (a former skating-rink) in Fulham, west London, and began selling and servicing motor cars. Obviously such enterprises called for extensive investment, but Rolls was a shrewd businessman, and not only did the venture prosper, it became all the more secure when Claude Johnson joined the company in 1904.

As for the man himself, Rolls was very much an individualist. Those who understood him accepted that he was not always easy to work for. He was not a socialite, and had few real friends. As a driver he was regarded as among the

Another view of the first Royce car, this time outside the entrance to 1A Cooke Street. Judging by the mud splattered on the front and rear guards, the vehicle was being used to its full potential. It is believed that the car shown underwent trials on 1 April 1904, but because Royce was superstitious, and wanted to avoid obvious connections with All Fool's Day, the date was in fact given as 31 March. On the far left of the picture can be seen a young boy who is taking a keen interest in the car. (Courtesy Rolls-Royce & Bentley Motor Cars Ltd)

finest, and he was certainly renowned for his engineering and mechanical skills, which often ensured he was the winner at motor sport events.

Henry Royce was born in 1863, the son of a miller, at Alwalton, near Peterborough. Aged nine when his father died, he was brought up by his mother and aunt in the best way they were able. Young Henry, nevertheless, was forced to sell newspapers to help the family funds, and at the age of 12 had received only three years schooling when he began work as a telegraph boy. He took an apprenticeship with the Great Northern Railway, which he was unable to complete because of financial hardship, and later sought a variety of engineering and electrical work, all of which provided a sound base on which to establish his own business manufacturing electrical equipment.

By 1894 F.H. Royce & Co. Ltd had sufficiently prospered to be valued at around a third of a million pounds in today's terms, a significant proportion having been earned from sub-contract work associated with the Manchester

Above: Mrs Minnie Royce and Mrs Smith aboard the third Royce car at the Royce home, Brae Cottage, Knutsford. This appears to be a somewhat posed photograph and is dated to around late autumn 1904. (Courtesy Sir Henry Royce Memorial Foundation)

Left: This is the first Rolls-Royce motor car, chassis 20150, pictured at Cooke Street in late 1905 or early 1906. (Courtesy Rolls-Royce & Bentley Motor Cars Ltd)

Ship Canal. Business expansion meant that work constructing electrical cranes was undertaken, and the company further evolved as Royce Ltd. As demand for Royce cranes increased, it became evident that the Cooke Street premises, and those adjoining in Blake Street, were no longer adequate, which prompted Royce to acquire additional premises, which he largely designed himself, at Manchester's Trafford Park.

Events around the world brought a difficult period of trading for Royce Ltd at around the turn of the century. Electrical equipment, cheaper than Royce could produce, was being

imported, mainly from Germany, and subsidiaries of American companies producing similar products were also being established in Britain. Not surprisingly Royce considered diversifying into other industries.

The difference in their social backgrounds did not prevent Rolls and Royce from having a deep respect for one another. That the two men got on well together is well documented, although it must be emphasised that without Edmunds's encouragement their meeting would not have taken place. There is further evidence that Rolls was so impressed with Royce and his cars that on his return to London he called on Claude Johnson in a rather excited state. Rolls,

Two views of chassis 20154 with either Dr Briggs, the car's first brief owner, or Kenneth Gillies, the car's second owner, at the wheel. The chassis had been prepared for display at the Paris Salon in 1904, and according to records was finished in primrose and black. The coachwork is by Barkers, a park phaeton. (Courtesy Rolls-Royce & Bentley Motor Cars Ltd)

The 10hp chassis 20162, as first registered on 13 January 1906. There is every reason to believe that this car was used by C.S. Rolls. In December the same year the car was sold to Paris E. Singer, who kept it until 1914, although the vehicle received a new lighter-weight body at the time of purchase. (Courtesy Rolls-Royce & Bentley Motor Cars Ltd)

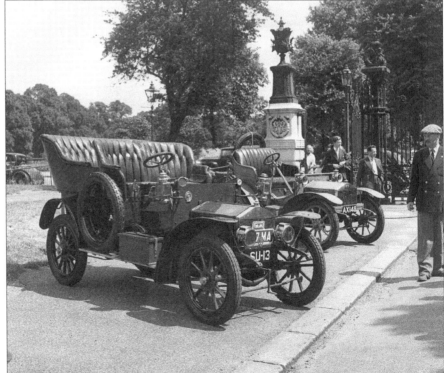

Chassis 20162 and 20165 pictured in Kensington Gardens at a Rolls-Royce Enthusiasts' Club meeting during the mid to late 1950s. (Courtesy Rolls-Royce & Bentley Motor Cars Ltd)

it seems, had not only found exactly the right product, but also an engineer of very high principles. Until making his acquaintance with Royce, Rolls had sold mainly foreign machines, although he had a strong desire to sell a British-made product as long as it was of suitably high quality. Rolls accepted

Pictured with 10hp chassis 20165 with Barker coachwork is Rolls-Royce employee Harry Fleck. The photograph was taken in 1946 when the car was donated to Rolls-Royce. Harry Fleck had delivered the car when new to Dr Sydney J. Gammell of Bielside in Scotland in 1907. (Courtesy Rolls-Royce & Bentley Motor Cars Ltd)

that he was unable to build cars himself to such excellence as he demanded, and thus realised that the future lay with a partnership with Royce.

The agreement that Rolls and Royce came to was that C.S. Rolls & Co. would have the sole selling rights to Royce's cars, which would thereafter be known and marketed as Rolls-Royces. The partnership had all the ingredients for a perfect recipe: Royce's engineering acumen, combined with Rolls's marketing skills and his many contacts throughout all levels of society, ensured that only the finest quality would be available to the most discerning of customers.

Chassis 20165 is seen outside the Blake Street entrance to the Cooke Street works after World War Two. The car alongside is the second production Silver Wraith, chassis WTA2. Silver Wraiths were built at Crewe. (Courtesy Rolls-Royce & Bentley Motor Cars Ltd)

Carrying the registration R 520, 10hp chassis 20167 is pictured with Eric Platford at the wheel; beside him is his bride. This was Henry Royce's own car, which he loaned to Platford for the duration of his honeymoon. Royce's generosity was typical of the man despite his often gruff manner. The photograph was taken in 1908 and of significance is the car's wide frame, which was lower-slung than other 10hp vehicles. (Courtesy Sir Henry Royce Memorial Foundation)

At the end of 1904 Royce produced a chassis layout for a three-cylinder 15hp car, of which six models were built, in contrast to the three prototype cars and 17 10hps. However, for Rolls-Royce the model proved to be not commercially viable.

Rolls's marketing prowess led to success on both sides of the Atlantic. In 1906 he attempted to break the 37.5-hour record from Monte Carlo to London, driving a four-cylinder 20hp car (chassis 40523), the most successful model of the very early Rolls-Royces. Rolls's travelling companions were Massac Buist, whom he had met at Cambridge and who later wrote the now sought after but rarely found *Rolls-Royce Memories*, and Cyril Durlacher, a company tester. The trio did break the record, but by a margin of only 90 seconds.

A Famous Radiator

Of particular significance in the history of the Rolls-Royce motor car is the design of the radiator. Royce cars, and indeed the first Rolls-Royces, did not carry the now esteemed radiator. There have, over the years, been various attempts to establish the origins of the design. There is no conclusive evidence, and it is possibly best left as something of an enigma. John Fasal and Bryan Goodman, joint authors of *The Edwardian Rolls-Royce*, record that some historians are of the opinion that the classical shape was influenced by Claude Johnson, while others believe it came about more technically, in order to improve water flow in the header tank. The late Ivan Evernden once suggested that the hot water from the cylinder heads was led to the top of the top tank and had to be dispersed across the upper of the radiator block in order to flow evenly downwards. By progressively reducing the cross section of the tank, a constant velocity of water within a minimal amount of material could be effected. Whatever the truth, the radiator shape, which is not entirely unique,

The three-cylinder 15hp was developed from 1904–5. Depicted here is chassis 23924 with Barker phaeton de luxe coachwork. The first owner of the vehicle was Dr C.B.E. Ware, headmaster of Eton, who was presented with the car on the occasion of his retirement in 1905 courtesy of Old Etonians, C.S. Rolls being one. (Courtesy Rolls-Royce & Bentley Motor Cars Ltd)

as similar styling was adopted by a number of manufacturers, is internationally recognised and universally associated with Rolls-Royce.

Pictured at the Derby works in around 1913 with Bert Day at the wheel, this 15hp car, chassis 26332, was first owned by Paris E. Singer of sewing-machine fame. Used as a works vehicle during World War One, the car was known to frequently backfire, which caused much concern to those living within the vicinity of the factory. (Courtesy Rolls-Royce & Bentley Motor Cars Ltd)

Relating to the radiator shape, Lord Hives, who eventually became chairman of Rolls-Royce after Royce's death, once wrote that while Royce had approved the design, he later came to detest it. There is no conclusive evidence of this, but it does add a further measure of embroidery to the intrigue that surrounds Rolls-Royce generally.

The sporting potential of Rolls-Royce was given a massive fillip when C.S. Rolls entered the Isle of Man Tourist Trophy events in 1905. Having competed in the Gordon Bennett Trials driving a Wolseley a little earlier in the year, Rolls was no stranger to the island, nor to the motorsport events for which it had already become renowned. Rolls was not encouraged by the thought of driving over-powered racing cars, and preferred Claude Johnson's vision (shared by the

The 20hp is noted as being the most successful of the early Rolls-Royces and featured two chassis types, the long wheelbase 'Heavy' and the shorter wheelbase 'Light'. Rolls-Royce, and C.S. Rolls in particular, became much associated with the Light 20hp in the Isle of Man Tourist Trophy events of 1905 and 1906. (Courtesy Rolls-Royce & Bentley Motor Cars Ltd)

Percy Northey drove his 20hp to second place in the 1905 Tourist Trophy event; alongside him is riding mechanic Cyril Durlacher. C.S. Rolls presented Northey with the picture in recognition of his fine performance in covering the 208 miles at a speed of 33¼ miles an hour without a stop. (Courtesy Rolls-Royce & Bentley Motor Cars Ltd)

C.S. Rolls's Light 20hp being refuelled before the start of the 1906 TT event. Rolls is seen supervising the delivery of the Shell Motor Spirit – petrol – and the scene is one of much activity. The car behind, number 5, is Percy Northey's. (Courtesy Rolls-Royce & Bentley Motor Cars Ltd)

influential Alfred Harmsworth) of using motor events to publicly test touring cars. Two Rolls-Royces were entered by Rolls, on the suggestion of Arthur Briggs (reported in the biography of Claude Johnson), an enthusiastic and sporting owner of a 20hp Landaulet. One of the cars was driven by Percy Northey, the other by Rolls. If Rolls-Royce cars had not already established themselves in the minds of the motorists of the day, the Tourist Trophy helped ensure that they did.

Left: Rolls appears to be in pensive mood before the start of the 1906 TT. (Courtesy Rolls-Royce & Bentley Motor Cars Ltd)

Above: Some controversy existed about Rolls-Royce's success in the 1905 Tourist Trophy event. There were doubts about whether the car was suitable to start on, and climb, steep gradients, and to quell any further argument Claude Johnson, who was to play a significant role in the fortunes of Rolls-Royce, demonstrated that the car was indeed capable of negotiating steep hills. (Courtesy Rolls-Royce & Bentley Motor Cars Ltd)

On Briggs's suggestion, Claude Johnson and Rolls had taken the prototype 20hp to the Isle of Man in May 1905, and the car performed extremely well. Claude Johnson knew the prototype machine as the 'Grey Ghost' and had arranged for an appropriately named plaque to be fixed to the vehicle's scuttle. It was this car which heralded the modified versions entered for the Tourist Trophy event. The chassis, being lighter and shorter than that of the Grey Ghost, gave rise to the nomenclature 'Light 20' to differentiate it from the original 'Heavy 20', which subsequently became known as the 'Long 20'. Among the many features of the Light 20 was its four-speed gearbox, which at the time was unusual, the top ratio acting as an overdrive.

There is little doubt that Rolls was nothing but confident that he and Percy Northey would be successful, not only in finishing the course, but also being well placed. The cars chosen to compete were Light 20s, the first of that type to appear from the Cooke Street works. Rolls was favourite to win the event, his efforts during practice having shown him to handle his motor car masterfully and achieve a fuel consumption of 26mpg at an average speed of 33mph. On race day Rolls had barely covered a quarter of a mile of the course when he was forced to retire because of

C.S.Rolls at the wheel of 26350B following his Isle of Man victory in 1906. Always modest, Rolls gave credit for winning the TT event not to himself or his co-driver, but to Henry Royce. When Royce heard of the success he gave the works personnel the rest of the day off with pay. (Courtesy Rolls-Royce & Bentley Motor Cars Ltd)

gearbox failure. There are several accounted reasons for the disaster, including sabotage. Percy Northey, however, fared somewhat better and achieved second place. Even here there was controversy: Northey was first across the finishing line, but the result was judged not only on position but also on timings and fuel consumption. The winner of the event was thus deemed to be John Napier, driving an Arrol-Johnston. The decision was challenged by Rolls, but his protest was not upheld by the judges.

Preparing for the 1906 Isle of Man Tourist Trophy event, two Light 20hp cars, 26350B (AX157) and 40523 (AX156), are pictured outside 'Woodlands', the location of the TT start. Eric Platford is at the wheel of AX157 and alongside him is C.S. Rolls. Percy Northey is driving AX156. (Courtesy Rolls-Royce & Bentley Motor Cars Ltd)

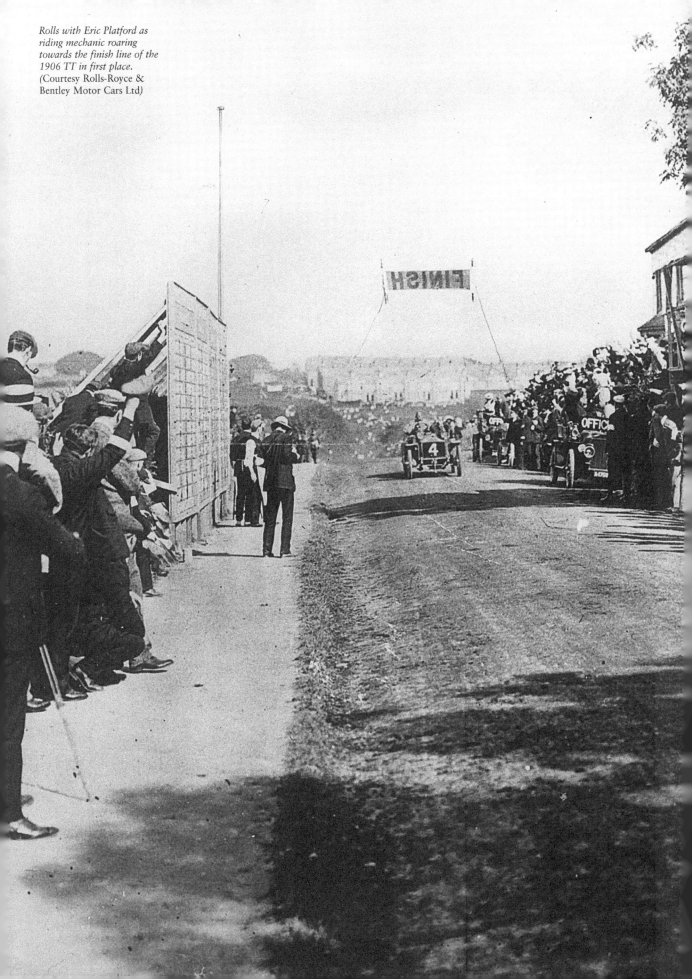

Rolls with Eric Platford as riding mechanic roaring towards the finish line of the 1906 TT in first place. (Courtesy Rolls-Royce & Bentley Motor Cars Ltd)

Development of the six-cylinder 30hp chassis began in early 1905 and this is a letter from C.S. Rolls & Co. to Edinburgh motor agent H. & D. Cleland, inviting them to attend a demonstration of the car on Thursday 28 September 1905. (Author's collection)

Any misgivings Rolls might have had at the time of the race were quickly forgotten, and in November 1905 he arranged a gala dinner at London's Trocadero. Guests of honour included Percy Northey and Henry Royce. Northey was congratulated for his excellent performance and for coming second, and Royce was applauded for his brilliant design and engineering. Claude Johnson, always the opportunist, had arranged for goggle-shape table place names to be available, and for menus to be printed on car-shaped cards.

The following year Rolls had his revenge and won the 1906 Isle of Man Tourist Trophy outright, again driving a Light 20. Percy Northey was also a

contender, and he too drove a Light 20. This time Northey suffered defeat, having to retire because of a broken front spring.

Forty 20hp cars were built, 21 utilising the heavy chassis, and 19 the light. Three further 20hp cars were constructed, these having eight-cylinder engines in 'V' formation. The V8 configuration was not used again by Rolls-Royce until 1959, when the company introduced the Silver Cloud II and Bentley S2 models. Known as the 'Landaulet *par excellence*' and 'Legalimit', the vehicles

Electric broughams found some favour in the early 1900s and to counter this Claude Johnson conceived the idea of a petrol-engined brougham. The motive power was a V8 20hp unit fitted low down in the chassis and virtually under the driver's feet. A car similar to that depicted was owned by Sir Alfred Harmsworth, who later became Lord Northcliffe, one of Rolls-Royce's most loyal and enthusiastic, albeit critical, customers. The term Legalimit came about because the 3,500cc engine was designed to propel the car at no more than 20mph, the speed limit then in force. (Courtesy Rolls-Royce & Bentley Motor Cars Ltd)

Right, middle: This 1906 30hp (chassis 60533) was supplied to the Hon. Mrs A. E. Assheton-Harbord. The driver is Harry Fleck, one of C.S. Rolls & Co's chauffeurs. The phaeton de luxe coachwork is by Barker. (Courtesy Rolls-Royce & Bentley Motor Cars Ltd)

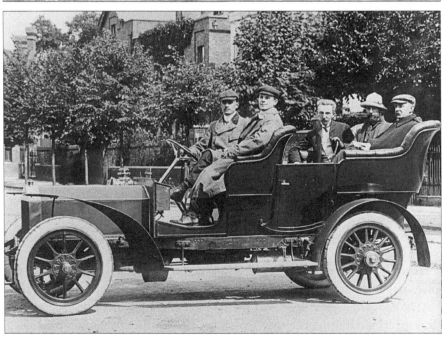

Right, bottom: When C.S. Rolls escorted visiting French naval officers he took them to Windsor using 23927, a 30hp short chassis. (Courtesy Rolls-Royce & Bentley Motor Cars Ltd)

were introduced in 1905, largely as a result of the preference of motorists at the time for electric broughams. What is significant about the project is that Charles Rolls and Claude Johnson had at one time, before the Rolls and Royce partnership, considered the manufacture of an electric carriage.

Lady Llangattock, C.S. Rolls's mother, preparing to leave South Lodge at the Hendre, the family home, for a ride in a 30hp. (Courtesy Rolls-Royce & Bentley Motor Cars Ltd)

The 30hp six-cylinder model dates from 1905, and 37 examples were produced (18 long chassis and 19 short chassis). When introduced, six-cylinder configured engines were a rarity, and it has to be said that the Cooke Street product did not always provide Rolls-Royce customers with the smoothness and sophistication that they had come to expect. Nevertheless, the 30hp did have significant merits, which were proved when Claude Johnson, a loyal advocate of the model, drove an example in the now famous Scottish Reliability Trials. In what was has been termed as the 'Battle of the Cylinders', readers of *The Automotor Journal* were entertained during the early part of 1906 with claims and counter-claims about the worthiness of four-cylinder engines compared to six-cylinder types. The dialogue continued for some time, with Captain H.P.P. Deasy, concessionaire for the Swiss 30-40hp four-cylinder Martini, challenging his car against a six-cylinder model of equal capacity. Johnson had become embroiled in the affair because he held very firm views on the merits of six-cylinder engines, and eventually accepted the challenge, which was staged as a performance trial and conducted under the auspices of the above-mentioned Scottish Reliability Trials.

The conditions of the event were such that both cars were subjected to in excess of 1,600 miles of demanding motoring, which included the round trip to Scotland as well as some 671 miles in the Scottish Highlands, timed sections and arduous hill-climbs. Claude Johnson was recognised as a fine driver, always getting the best from a car with minimum effort, and he would have welcomed the fact that Percy Northey had also entered the trials driving a 20hp Rolls-Royce, thus bolstering the company's presence. The trial was adjudicated by members of the London Stock Exchange and observed by the Automobile Club, the result being that Claude Johnson's car was the only six-cylinder vehicle not to lose any marks. Declared as the winner of the 'Battle of the Cylinders', Johnson had amassed 396 points for reliability, silence of running and absence of shock and vibration, and had experienced only a single involuntary stop in order to adjust the car's footbrake.

During the formative years of Rolls-Royce it was the 30hp that did much to promote the company's image for luxury travel and vehicle reliability. Claude Johnson was in his element, and went to great lengths to demonstrate the car's prowess, especially to quell criticisms of its performance. When it was suggested that the 30hp was too large a car to turn in London streets, a £10 wager was laid by Claude Johnson, who proved that the car was particularly agile by turning in a 40ft roadway with some 8ft to spare. When the car's climbing ability was called into question, Johnson tackled the renowned hill up to the Cat and Fiddle in the Peak District. Not only did the car drive up the hill in top gear without having to change ratios, it carried four passengers.

Contemporary publicity material as published in The Autocar. *(Courtesy Autocar, and Rolls-Royce & Bentley Motor Cars Ltd)*

CHAPTER TWO

NIGHTINGALE ROAD

IT WAS Claude Johnson that instigated the move from Cooke Street to new premises, having successfully convinced Rolls and Royce of the need to do so. Moreover, Johnson had envisaged that moving to a purpose-built factory would carry prestige. Again, Rolls and Royce were in agreement. Forefront in Claude Johnson's mind, and that of Royce, was the need for a facility to produce a new car, the 40/50hp, (of which more later) and a policy of producing a single model instead of several different types.

The home of Britain's motor industry was mainly in the Midlands; Coventry and the surrounding area in particular. Pockets of the industry were found around the country, one of them in Manchester, but Claude Johnson considered it important that Rolls-Royce should exist away from the traditional motor-building lands. There was nothing sinister about this view: Johnson believed that while there was a pool of labour skilled in the coachbuilding and motor engineering industries available, wage rates were higher in the Midlands than in Manchester, and as a result some of the company's highly proficient personnel might be lost to other firms.

Johnson took it upon himself to look for the most appropriate alternative location away from the established motor-building areas. There were several requirements to be fulfilled, such as land prices, availability of skilled labour,

The Rolls-Royce works as portrayed on a plan dated 1907, a year before the official opening. The inset shows the original buildings, ands illustrates how the Nightingale Road factory expanded over the years. The main office block can be seen on the larger plan, to the left of the first-built premises. (Courtesy Sir Henry Royce Memorial Foundation)

supplies of raw materials, communications, transportation and distribution facilities along with adequate water and power supplies. A number of towns and cities were evaluated, the sifting process taking a considerable amount of time and effort. Manchester was an obvious consideration, as the home of Rolls-Royce, and before it, Royce Ltd, makers of cranes and electrical equipment at its factory at Trafford Park. Nearby Stretford was considered to have some potential, until a negative site assessment made such a choice unlikely.

Bradford, across the Pennines, was suggested

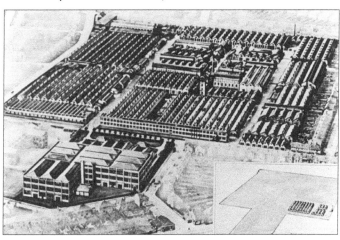

The official opening day, 9 July 1908. An auspicious occasion, the event was attended by some 70 guests, who included local dignitaries as well as personalities from the motor industry. Lord Montagu of Beaulieu conducted the opening ceremony, and he is seen aboard the leading car, the Silver Rogue, which is driven by Eric Platford. (Courtesy Sir Henry Royce Memorial Foundation)

by Claude Johnson's friend Arthur Briggs, who offered to provide suitable land on which to build a factory. Nottingham, where industrial growth was being encouraged, was a city keen to welcome Rolls-Royce, and some interest was shown towards Macclesfield, but it was Leicester that Claude Johnson most

Another view of the guests arriving at Nightingale Road on 9 July 1908. In the centre can be seen Henry Royce who is wearing a cap; ahead of him is Claude Johnson, and behind him is Mrs Assheton-Harbord. (Courtesy Sir Henry Royce Memorial Foundation)

Guests being conducted around the Nightingale Road Works on opening day. Note the selection of Rolls-Royce cars parked alongside the workshops. (Courtesy Sir Henry Royce Memorial Foundation)

This is the extent of the Rolls-Royce factory in 1908. Number one gate can be seen, and it is through this entrance that guests were directed to the opening ceremony, which was held in the building to the right. These buildings remain an integral part of the factory today. (Courtesy Sir Henry Royce Memorial Foundation)

favoured. Had it not been for a late and surprise representation by officials from Derby Town Council, Leicester might well have been the ultimate choice. What Derby offered was too good an opportunity to disregard: not only did council officials propose suitable land at a most affordable price, but gave assurances regarding additional land for future development. The package was far reaching, and there was a commitment to supply electricity at advantageous tariffs under a long-term agreement, and provision was made for all other mains services: gas, water and sewerage.

The Derby proposal thus far was probably sufficient to clinch a deal with Rolls-Royce. There were, nevertheless, further advantages which far outweighed any rival bid. As well as building roads, there was provision for a railway siding into the factory site, and the council was willing to undertake the installation of electrical services and equipment, including the necessary powerful motors, on an economic rental basis.

There were more good reasons to favour Derby. The local authority intimated that it would be unopposed to the building of homes for Rolls-Royce workers, some of whom would transfer from Manchester. Henry Royce was particularly enthusiastic about moving to Derby for rather more fundamental reasons: rates of pay were lower than those in Manchester, and although he proposed maintaining paying Manchester wages, there was every reason to expect that personnel would be reluctant to seek employment elsewhere. Royce, of course, had the satisfaction of knowing that his employees were the most highly skilled anywhere, and that by turning out a strictly limited number of cars of the highest quality, the company had established a

This view of the works at around the time of the opening ceremony shows the famous chimney with its R-R monogram, a noted Derby landmark. The perimeter road served as part of the works' test track. (Courtesy Sir Henry Royce Memorial Foundation)

The Rolls-Royce test track in the early days of the factory. The scene is almost leisurely in appearance, but it gives a clue about the relatively desolate surroundings of what was once the Osmaston Estate. (Courtesy Sir Henry Royce Memorial Foundation)

particular reputation. Derby, which had been the pioneering centre of the silk industry in Britain, also prided itself on having a ready and skilled labour market courtesy of the railway locomotive works which were already established in the town.

A Visit to Derby

In his biography of Claude Johnson, Wilton J. Oldham recounts the day that Tom Smith, C.S. Rolls's chauffeur, was summoned to Conduit Street with the request to bring Rolls's Laundalette to the London showroom. This was soon after Rolls had returned from a trip to America in December 1906, when he had successfully appointed an agent to sell Rolls-Royce motor cars. Arriving

The main commercial block of the factory was not completed until 1912. In planning the building Royce was keen that personnel should not spend time peering out of the windows, and therefore had them positioned at a height to make this difficult. (Courtesy Sir Henry Royce Memorial Foundation)

The architect of the Derby factory was Henry Royce, who is seen in this photograph relaxing at his home at Quarndon with his black Labrador Rajah in around 1910. The Silver Ghost is chassis 1200, a Derby trials car which Royce used personally on a number of occasions. (Courtesy Sir Henry Royce Memorial Foundation)

For years Royce had experienced
poor health that prevented him
from working at Derby, so instead
he worked from his homes on the
south coast of England and at Le
Canadel in southern France.
(Courtesy Sir Henry Royce
Memorial Foundation)

at Conduit Street, Tom Smith was met by Rolls, together with Claude Johnson and Henry Royce. His orders were to drive to Derby by the most direct and quickest route, and when they arrived at the outskirts of the south side of the city he was told to find Nightingale Road. There the chauffeur found a newly made road amid flat and barren country. The three passengers got out of the car and walked around gazing at the landscape while having some heavy discussion before eventually getting back into the car.

Tom Smith's orders were then to drive to the Midland Railway Station. Claude Johnson, Rolls and Royce had decided to take the train back to London for a more speedy return journey, and Tom Smith drove the car back to the capital alone. The event clearly illustrates journey times by road at the beginning of the 20th century compared to those by rail. Tom Smith may have already realised the reason for the journey to Derby, but nevertheless Rolls confided to his chauffeur that it was to Derby that the company was intending to move.

Negotiations between the Derby authority and Rolls-Royce proceeded quickly. On 6 April 1907 an announcement to the effect that the company had elected to move to land on what was the Osmaston Estate at Derby was published in *The Autocar*, there being every indication that development of the 12-acre site would begin immediately. It did just that, and, as recorded in the *Derby Mercury*, the foundations were commenced the same month.

Behind the scenes at Cooke Street, in Rolls's office at Conduit Street, and on behalf of Claude Johnson, some hectic discussions regarding company finance had been taking place. The cramped conditions of the Royce works had for some time been recognised as being a limiting factor in developing new models, and for Claude Johnson's vision of a one-model policy to materialise, serious changes in the way Rolls-Royce was financed were necessary. Claude Johnson believed that for Rolls-Royce to survive, the company had to market just one model rather than several, each having different chassis types. Some 30 years later, W.A. Robotham, head of chassis design, held exactly the same opinion when forecasting production requirements and finances.

To appreciate the financial situation it is necessary to return to the early days of the Rolls-Royce motor car. Accepting that the future of C.S. Rolls & Co. lay with closer liaison with Royce Ltd, Rolls and Johnson took the advice of A.H. Briggs to forge an amalgamation with Henry Royce. The advantages of such a relationship were clearly apparent to Rolls and Claude Johnson, and when they approached Royce they found him to be quite agreeable. Royce, after all, was supplying all his output of Rolls-Royces to C.S. Rolls & Co., and greater affiliation seemed the inevitable route.

Left top and middle: Inside the test house at Nightingale Road. A 40/50hp is seen on the chassis dynamometer, which registered power at the rear wheels. The power was measured by engaging the rear wheels with rollers, the chains affording the necessary security. Sadly the identity of the two fitters has not been traced. (Courtesy Sir Henry Royce Memorial Foundation)

Above: Within a year of Rolls's death Royce was taken seriously ill and was prevented from returning to Derby except for on one occasion. Claude Johnson was often away from Derby for lengthy periods, and in his absence some highly skilled engineers took on the burden of the daily running of the factory. Arthur Wormald became general works manager, a position that warranted him being appointed to the Rolls-Royce board. He had joined F.H. Royce & Co. in 1904 and stayed with the company until his death in 1936. (Courtesy Sir Henry Royce Memorial Foundation)

Rolls-Royce Limited

A new company, registered as Rolls-Royce Limited, was formed on 16 March 1906 with a nominal capital of £60,000. A little in excess of half the capital, £35,000, was in preference shares; ordinary shares accounted for £22,000, and deferred shares amounted to £5,000. C.S. Rolls & Co. held £10,000-worth of preference shares and £5,000-worth of deferred shares, the latter being later converted to ordinary shares. In establishing Rolls-Royce Limited, all of C.S. Rolls & Co.'s assets and business were taken

Left: Tom Haldenby began his career with Royce Ltd in 1900, when he was an apprentice at Cooke Street. When C.S. Rolls & Co. was absorbed by Rolls-Royce, Haldenby became manager at Lillie Hall before moving to Nightingale Road in 1913, where he worked under Ernest Hives. When Arthur Wormald was appointed general manager, Tom Haldenby became his assistant, eventually rising to become general manager. (Courtesy Sir Henry Royce Memorial Foundation)

Chassis testing both inside the works and outside on the test track was routine business at Nightingale Road. Sometimes there were mishaps, as seen here – a 40/50hp has overturned. (Courtesy Sir Henry Royce Memorial Foundation)

The foundry at Nightingale Road prior to World War One. The standards were exacting, as they have always been. At the far end of the building can be seen the furnace. (Courtesy Sir Henry Royce Memorial Foundation)

over. As far as Royce Ltd was concerned, it was only the car making business that was absorbed, and the parent company manufacturing cranes and electrical equipment continued separately until after Henry Royce's death in 1933. The assets of Royce Ltd were eventually acquired by H.G. Morris of Loughborough, who continued the Royce crane business for some further years. Royce Ltd received 7,000 preference shares, together with all the ordinary shares and debentures, which were valued at £8,500, this being in consideration of the car-making equipment at Cooke Street.

On formation of Rolls-Royce Limited, Ernest Claremont, formerly Chairman of Royce Ltd, was elected financial adviser; Rolls was appointed technical managing director, Royce was chief engineer and works director, and Claude Johnson commercial managing director. John De Looze was appointed company secretary and retained the post until taking retirement in 1943. Along with Ernest Claremont, De Looze was one of the prime figures in the success of Royce Ltd, and later Rolls-Royce Limited. He joined Royce in 1893 as cashier and accountant, and the following year was appointed company secretary.

It could be supposed that Rolls-Royce, with its reputation for producing fine motor cars and, later, aero-engines, would, at Cooke Street, have been equipped with the best tooling then available. Interestingly this was not the case: Royce Ltd was constantly under-capitalised, and C.W. Morton mentions in his *A History of Rolls-Royce Motor Cars* that the factory comprised 'The finest collection of second-hand rattleguts machinery in Manchester.'

The urgency of establishing a new factory with the most up-to-date machine

tools, and securing the finances required to fund the project, meant that the decision was taken to provide shareholders and the general public with the opportunity of purchasing a further £100,000 worth of shares. In doing this, the capital of Rolls-Royce Limited would be increased to £200,000.

The period in question was one of boom for Britain's fledgling motor companies, the motor industry having been given a boost by recent and long-awaited relaxations in the law. There were some highly successful enterprises, but there were also many failures. Having carefully studied the trading results of other car

The car repair department at Derby in around 1912. On the extreme right is Fred Pitt, who is accompanied by his gang standing around a 40/50hp Silver Ghost. The car can be seen minus its coachwork, and it was customary when testing the chassis for the driver to sit on wooden boxes placed on the frame. (Courtesy Sir Henry Royce Memorial Foundation)

manufacturers, including Daimler, Argyll, Napier and Panhard et Levassor, Claude Johnson was convinced that the time was right to attract an enthusiastic response, and advised Rolls-Royce directors accordingly. Today it seems unthinkable that the key players in Rolls-Royce, other than C.S. Rolls, were largely unknown to the wider public. Had the company had a recognised figurehead, the outcome of the flotation might have been very different. To add to what will be seen as a negative response to the flotation, investors had, by the closing weeks of 1906, become largely suspicious of motor manufacturers, especially the smaller companies, of which Rolls-Royce was one. On too many occasions financiers had speculated in motor firms only to witness shortlived trading and the loss of their investment. The whole subject of financing the motor trade, and a strong warning about its pitfalls, was expressed in *The Economist*. Exacerbating matters still further, the financial journals of the day did not cast the prospectus of Rolls-Royce in a good light, warning investors about vague propositions and weak appeal.

The Rolls-Royce prospectus gives some clue about the expected remuneration of company directors. Henry Royce received £1,250 per annum and additionally earned 4 per cent of the profits in excess of £10,000. Rolls and Johnson received somewhat less than Royce, each being awarded £750 per annum together with 4 per cent of the surplus profits. Ernest Claremont was paid £250 per annum along with 2 per cent of the surplus profits.

When Rolls-Royce shares were offered to the public in early December, subscriptions amounted to £41,000, far short of the £50,000 which had been stipulated as a minimum. Of the sum subscribed, £10,000 was attributed to Rolls. Had the minimum subscription not been attained, the flotation would have had to be abandoned, and the monies returned to investors.

It was to A.H. Briggs that John De Looze appealed. Having travelled to Harrogate to canvass Briggs, the wealthy businessman and possibly the greatest exponent of the Rolls-Royce motor car, along with Alfred Harmsworth and Henry Edmunds, returned with a cheque for £10,000, and thus saved the company from under-subscription. Rolls-Royce acknowledged Briggs's generosity by offering him a seat on the board, which he accepted and retained until his death in 1919. A final mark of the company's recognition of his generosity over many years was that the annual report which appeared after Briggs's death was edged in black, on the insistence of De Looze.

Claude Johnson was keen to have elected to the Rolls-Royce board another

The test shop pictured in around 1913. As with many of the photographs of the period, this was taken at a time of limited personnel activity. For testing purposes the chassis were fitted with temporary 'slave' seats to enable testing to be conducted. (Courtesy Sir Henry Royce Memorial Foundation)

well-known personality whom, it was anticipated, would have considerable influence. That person was Captain the Lord Herbert Scott DSO, an officer with the Irish Guards, the son of the Duke of Buccleuch and cousin to Lord Montagu. Lord Herbert Scott accepted the invitation, resigned his commission with the army, and thus joined the esteemed sales team of a prestigious company.

With the name of Rolls-Royce becoming more and more associated with quality and reliability, the need arose to increase production and cater for demand. Rolls-Royce, as noted by the media when reviewing the share flotation prospectus, was perceived as a low-volume manufacturer, and with production averaging three cars per month, who could argue? For 1907 Rolls-Royce forecast doubling production to six or seven cars per month for ten months, but even this figure was considerably fewer than the 200 cars a year company directors had advocated. The new factory, when complete, would have to accommodate building at least 16 or 17 cars a month and have sufficient capacity to increase production when required.

The site of the new Rolls-Royce factory having been finally decided, amid loud protestations by George Mawby, Leicester's borough surveyor, who was convinced that the company would elect to move to his town (a site at Abbey Road), and who had achieved much to make this possible, construction work commenced early in 1907. It was Royce who was appointed to oversee the building and preparation of the works, and to this end he undertook to design

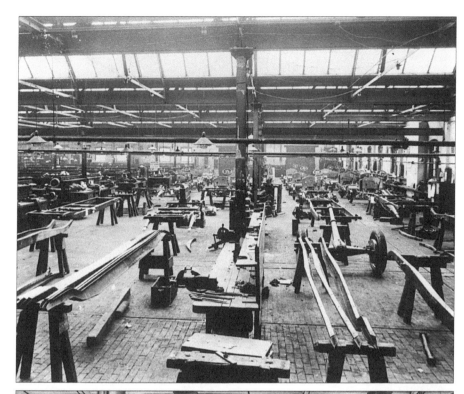

The chassis erecting shop in 1913, showing a number of 40/50hp cars in the process of being built. In the foreground chassis are in the preliminary stages of construction, and in the foreground can be seen those in a more advanced state of readiness. (Courtesy Sir Henry Royce Memorial Foundation)

Another view of the chassis erecting shop taken at the same time as the preceding photograph. The chassis on the left are nearly complete while those on the right are awaiting fitment of tyres. (Courtesy Sir Henry Royce Memorial Foundation)

and lay out the workshops, as well as specifying the types of equipment that were needed.

Royce's efforts preparing the Derby factory meant him moving from Manchester in order to devote his time to the project. Renting a house at Quarndon, to the north of Derby, Royce, his wife Minnie and her niece Violet Punt (whom the Royces later adopted), moved to 'The Knoll'. To avoid

The commercial office at Nightingale Road on 1 January 1913. The main office block had just been finished and the commercial office was nearly ready to move into the new premises. The staff on the left of the picture, front to back, are identified as Ben Pope, Jim Martin, Joe Lomas, Kilner, Claton and Lomas. In the centre, again front to back, are Sanderson, Florrie Pickles, Crossfield, Dickenson and Ritson. Far right can be seen Miss Hanlon, Robinson, John De Looze, Miss Blatchley, Aitcheson and Geare.

working seven days a week, the family also acquired a lodge, known as 'Seacote', at Overstrand on the Norfolk coast near Cromer, where relaxing weekends were spent. It was possibly at Minnie Royce's insistence – influenced no doubt by the concerns of Ernest Claremont and John De Looze – that Royce took regular rest periods. For some years he had suffered ill-health, and working around the clock, as Royce was often tempted to do, was unwise. In typical Royce fashion the construction of the factory progressed at great speed, Royce himself being involved in every aspect of the building programme.

Building the factory

Within nine months of building work having commenced, the first phase of the Derby factory was complete, the floor space of the premises accounting for some 1 acres. In comparison to the then trends in industrial architecture, the Derby premises were unusual, and the workshops were as spacious, light and airy as later fashions and regulations dictated. The area of glass used in the roofing amounted to half the area of the flooring, and the fact that it had a north-east aspect, and was set at an angle of 45 degrees, allowed in the best possible daylight. As might be expected of an engineer with extensive electrical engineering experience, the artificial lighting, using arc and incandescent lamps, was the most modern of the day.

Royce insisted that where possible local labour be used in the construction of the factory. The company assigned to build the works was Derby-based Messrs Handysides and Co., the firm recognised for such structures as the Olympia exhibition centre in London, and the new Victoria, Liverpool Street

and Charing Cross rail-way stations.

Plans completed before the opening of the factory show the original single-storey premises divided into two distinct sections, one having a high risk of fire, the other having a much reduced risk. The former comprised the smith shop, foundry, hardening shop and test area; the latter the machine shops, stores and erecting bay. Within the factory an internal trolley network connected departments, and the maze of lines were linked by means of turntables positioned at strategic points. Additionally, the principal factory production areas were fed by overhead conveyors. The first workshops to be constructed were those adjacent to Nightingale Road, and surviving drawings show shop No.1, the chassis erecting bay, repair garage, foundry and lavatory. In total area these workshops alone gave double the floor area of the Cooke Street factory. The site also included a vehicle test track with banked corners, a facility which, at the time, was forward-looking.

Contemporary media reports praised the efficient layout of the works, which allowed for the fabrication of virtually every component. The fact that facilities existed for what were viewed as pretty complex manufacturing processes obviously made an impression, and the installation of automatic tools and overhead motors was the cause of much comment. Of some interest is the space allocated on the drawings for a two-storey office block which was to front the factory and be parallel with Nightingale Road. Devised by Royce at the outset of planning, the offices were not built until 1912. Royce, conscious that he wanted to avoid personnel peering out of the office windows and daydreaming when they should be working, insisted that the windows were positioned at a sufficient height to deter such occurrences!

As the workshops were completed, so the transfer of operations from Cooke Street was methodically undertaken. The entire process took something like a year to accomplish, throughout which time there was no break in vehicle production. When finalised, arrangements were made for a grand official opening, which took place on 9 July 1908.

The task of arranging the ceremony was, not surprisingly, assigned to Claude Johnson, for this was exactly the type of event that he excelled in organising. There is every reason to believe that the ceremony was to have been held at an earlier date, but was delayed because Rolls-Royce had entered two vehicles in the International Touring Car Trials. By delaying the official opening, Rolls-Royce would have the advantage of knowing the cars' fate or success.

The Opening Ceremony

Claude Johnson invited John Montagu of Beaulieu to perform the opening ceremony, and it can be presumed that his cousin, Lord Herbert Scott, played

The Alpine Trials proved to be successful for Rolls-Royce, and were conducted by Ernest Hives, who is seen here with fellow racing drivers A.J. Hancock and Parsons. Hives was at the time heavily involved with the experimental department and was furthering his career to become general manager of Rolls-Royce. (Courtesy Sir Henry Royce Memorial Foundation)

'Royce, conscious that he wanted to avoid personnel peering out of the office windows... insisted that the windows were positioned at a sufficient height to deter such occurrences.'

Maurice Olley and Albert Elliot, pictured at Le Canadel, Royce's home in the south of France, driving a small French tourer in 1913. Olley had joined Rolls-Royce in 1912 as a jig and tool designer and was instrumental in much of the pioneering work on Rolls-Royce's first aero-engine, the Eagle. Elliott also joined the company in 1912 when he was recruited from Napier. Elliot became Royce's principal assistant during World War One, and after Royce's death he was appointed chief engineer. (Courtesy Sir Henry Royce Memorial Foundation)

an essential role in making this possible. To imagine the opening ceremony as a huge gala occasion with hundreds of guests would be a far cry from the truth. H. Massac Buist, writing in *Rolls-Royce Memories,* captured the sense of the event quite succinctly. 'It was not a stage-managed affair', he wrote, 'but as a quite informal little gathering in a room, followed by an inspection of the Works'.

The ceremony was attended by some 70 or so guests. Local dignitaries included the Mayor of Derby Alderman A. Simpson, Alderman J. Hart JP, Alderman Winter and Alderman Sir Edward Ann JP. Arthur Longden, chairman of the Derby development committee, was present, along with its secretary A.D. Farnsworth. There were guests from the world of motoring, such as John Siddeley (Wolseley), Earl Russell (Humber) and Ernest Instone (Daimler). Rolls-Royce customers were invited, those present including the Hon. Mrs Assheton-Harboard the enthusiastic aeronaut, J. Blamires, Henry Edmunds and the aforementioned H. Massac Buist.

Speakers other than John Montagu were Charles Rolls, Henry Royce and Claude Johnson. Of Rolls, Montagu spoke of 'the most skilled driver'; Johnson was 'the man of business', and he referred to Royce as 'the mechanical genius'. Montagu, no doubt inspired by Claude Johnson's aptitude for publicity, extolled the Rolls-Royce as the best car in the world, and told his audience that he had just ordered a model for himself. This is exactly the type of publicity that Claude Johnson rejoiced in receiving: in actual fact John Montagu already had considerable experience of Rolls-Royce motor cars and had been running a

Light 20 for some two years. Nevertheless, the accolade was music to the ears of those journalists who were present. With the pressing of a switch, which turned on the electric power to the factory, John Montagu declared the works open.

For the work force at 'Royce's', the name by which the Derby works was forever known, and still is by those folk who remember the works of earlier years, 9 July was an auspicious occasion. For months, the task of preparing for the move to Derby from Manchester, and transferring production, was the cause of much concern to those on the shop floor. Those principally involved were Eric Platford and Arthur Wormald, the latter becoming works manager and a director of the company after 1912.

It was Arthur Wormald to whom Royce entrusted the daily running of Cooke Street while he was absent preparing the Derby site. Wormald was a highly skilled engineer and tool-maker, and Royce had secured his appointment from the Westinghouse Company in 1904. He was a key figure in producing cars in the formative years of Royce and Rolls-Royce, and was fundamental in providing much of the necessary tooling.

By nature, Arthur Wormald demonstrated an element of cunning perception, a personality characteristic which assured him a leading role in the fortunes of Rolls-Royce well into the inter-war years. There has been discussion that he surrounded himself with a management team that was both loyal and ruthless, but history has shown Wormald to have been particularly receptive to the workforce, and during his tenure of office industrial relations at Rolls-Royce had never been better.

With the official opening of the Derby factory consigned to history, the works proceeded to produce the 40/50hp model, one of the most successful motor cars of all time.

Rolls-Royce workers leaving the works at the end of a shift sometime before the onset of World War One. The number of employees at Nightingale Road steadily increased from some 400 in 1908 to around 800 in 1911. In 1913–14 around 1,000 people were engaged at the Derby factory. (Courtesy Sir Henry Royce Memorial Foundation)

CHAPTER THREE

SILVER GHOSTS AND ARMOURED CARS

THE SILVER GHOST is probably the best-known car in motoring history. There have been other cars that, arguably, are equally as famous, but few share the Rolls-Royce's charisma. The Silver Ghost has been a powerful marketing tool for Rolls-Royce, and it is remarkable that the car, chassis 60551 and registered AX 201, returned to company ownership in 1948 when it was reacquired from its then owner, the Hanbury family of Castle Malwood near Lyndhurst, Hampshire. The car had originally been sold to Daniel Hanbury of Eaton Square, London, in 1908, following its use as a trials car under the direction of Claude Johnson.

Although the name Silver Ghost is applied to the 40/50hp model in general, there was in fact only the one car that was bestowed with the appellation. Silver Ghost was extensively and unofficially used until the announcement of the Phantom models in May 1925 (the Phantom was otherwise known as the New Phantom, and later designated Phantom I on introduction of the Phantom II) after which Rolls-Royce authorised the title's wider application.

The concept of the 40/50hp dates to the formative years of Rolls-Royce and the 30hp car. Working closely with Henry Royce, Claude Johnson had become seriously concerned that the 30hp's performance would be severely compromised when fitted with large and heavy coachwork. It was Montague Graham-White, a respected coachwork designer and engineer, who had alerted Claude Johnson's attention to the potential problem, predicting criticism that the car was underpowered. During the Edwardian era it was usual to travel with an abundance of luggage together with household staff, a maid and valet at least, and therefore motor cars capable of accommodating as many as seven people were not uncommon.

The question of coachwork styles was just one of a number of problems that Claude Johnson and Henry Royce had to face. One in particular was that

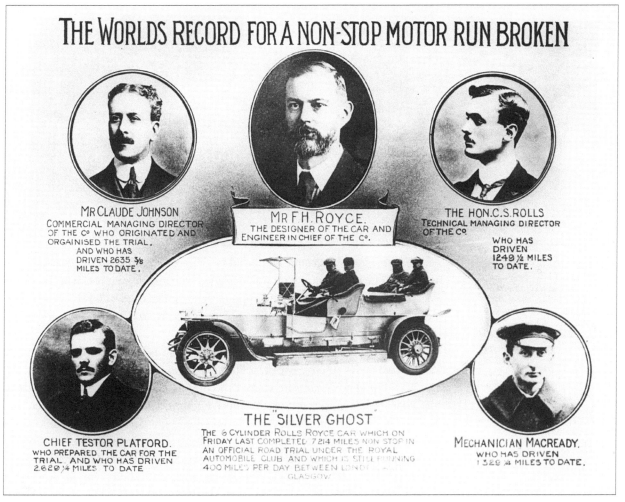

THE WORLDS RECORD FOR A NON-STOP MOTOR RUN BROKEN

MR CLAUDE JOHNSON
COMMERCIAL MANAGING DIRECTOR
OF THE Cº WHO ORIGINATED AND
ORGANISED THE TRIAL,
AND WHO HAS
DRIVEN 2635 ⅜
MILES TO DATE.

MR F.H. ROYCE.
THE DESIGNER OF THE CAR AND
ENGINEER IN CHIEF OF THE Cº.

THE HON.C.S.ROLLS
TECHNICAL MANAGING DIRECTOR
OF THE Cº
WHO HAS
DRIVEN
1249 ½ MILES
TO DATE.

CHIEF TESTOR PLATFORD.
WHO PREPARED THE CAR FOR THE
TRIAL, AND WHO HAS DRIVEN
2620¼ MILES TO DATE

THE "SILVER GHOST"
THE 6 CYLINDER ROLLS ROYCE CAR WHICH ON
FRIDAY LAST COMPLETED 7214 MILES NON STOP IN
AN OFFICIAL ROAD TRIAL UNDER THE ROYAL
AUTOMOBILE CLUB AND WHICH IS STILL RUNNING
400 MILES PER DAY BETWEEN LONDON
GLASGOW

MECHANICIAN MACREADY.
WHO HAS DRIVEN
1328¼ MILES TO DATE.

Royce, who was committed to complete thoroughness of design, was producing an increasingly diverse range of components, which detracted from his original aim of making parts interchangeable wherever possible. Modifications to the existing chassis ranges were constantly being made in the interests of improving technology, and with discussions about a new six-cylinder car on-going, it was Claude Johnson who grasped the idea of employing a single model, partly as a means of economy, but mostly to increase resource efficiency.

Claude Johnson's ideas did not materialise immediately. Royce, having designed a new chassis, was intent on having at least two examples ready to be exhibited at the 1906 London Motor Show. With many other projects vying for his time, it is something of a surprise that he managed to complete so much. By late summer, with drawings complete, work began in the crowded Cooke Street works preparing engine castings. In view of the difficulties that he had experienced with the 30hp engine, Royce designed the 40/50hp engine with two blocks of three cylinders, in contrast to the 30hp's three blocks of two. Seven main bearings were utilised, these being in the upper half of the crankcase, and oil under pressure fed directly to the main, big end and little end bearings. With a power output of 48hp at 1700rpm, the engine's mounting design was unusual in having only three bearing points: the one at the front was designed to insulate the aluminium crank chamber from the torsional stresses

The Silver Ghost, the name given to the twelfth 40/50hp model, chassis 60551, is probably the best known of all Rolls-Royces, and as a publicity tool for the company its value is priceless. The 40/50hp was unveiled at the 1906 London Motor Show and for Rolls-Royce represented a 'one-model' policy which lasted until 1922. As for the 40/50hp, it continued in production until 1925. It was 60551, carrying the registration number AX 201, which completed a 15,000-mile endurance record in 1907, and those personalities primarily connected with the event are shown in this piece of publicity material. (Courtesy Rolls-Royce & Bentley Motor Cars Ltd)

of the frame, and was centrally placed to affix to the centre of the chassis cross-member. The 40/50hp engine was designed to be more reliable than the 30hp: each of the cylinder blocks incorporated the cylinder heads, and the valves were positioned alongside the cylinders and operated by rocking levers via a single camshaft.

For the 1906 Motor Show Montague Graham-White was commissioned to design two styles of coachwork, a Pullman Limousine and a Sports Tourer, for the 40/50hp. The Limousine caused the designer immense difficulties because the coachbuilder, none other the most highly respected firm of Barker, had interpreted his drawings in a way that horrified him. Because the roofline of the car had been raised to a height that would have allowed gentlemen wearing top hats to enter the vehicle, Graham-White considered the resulting carriage to be extremely ugly. In retrospect, few Rolls-Royce enthusiasts would now share Graham-White's disappointment in the design; it was in fact the most splendid of motor cars, with its ornate fenestral detailing and clerestory roof.

The Barker and Graham-White incident leads nicely into another aspect of Rolls-Royce history. Rolls appears to have negotiated with Barker to conduct the sole selling of the coachbuilder's output for R-R chassis. Despite Montague Graham-White's distaste for Barker's efforts concerning the Pullman Limousine, the designer nevertheless remained committed to both Rolls-Royce and the coachbuilder. There is evidence that Rolls, Royce and Claude Johnson had investigated the possibility of establishing their own coachbuilding business, or at least arranging for Rolls-Royce to have its own in-house coachwork facilities. Obviously this would have had to have been a most specialised undertaking, and something which would have undoubtedly called for huge investment. Claude Johnson would have looked at the costings and requirements very closely, and there is every indication that, given Rolls-Royce's financial situation, the venture would have been too great to consider, especially at the time when the Nightingale Road factory was being proposed.

Montague Graham-White's Barker Pullman Limousine, built on chassis 60539, the first of the 40/50hp chassis, was highly regarded and, as well as being illustrated in the 1907 Rolls-Royce catalogue and referred to as a 'Pullman-de-Luxe', was used by the company as a showroom car at Conduit Street. When displayed at the 1906 London Motor Show, the car was without its engine. The precise reason for exhibiting a 'dummy' car is unknown, but speculation is that the engine was either unfinished or left unfitted because of time constraints.

Claude Johnson and the One-Model Policy

The 1906 Motor Show and the interest that was shown in the 40/50hp cars was, for Claude Johnson, the deciding factor in favour of his one-model policy. There is no doubt that the 40/50hp stole the show, and customers responded by swamping the Rolls-Royce stand with orders which, in reality, the company could not readily fulfil. By discontinuing the 20hp and 30hp models along with the V8, the factory was able to accommodate solely the 40/50hp, which Claude Johnson rightly believed to be the finest car then available.

Leaving the technical side of perfecting the 40/50hp to Henry Royce, Claude Johnson got on with promoting the car in the manner he knew best. A trials car was allocated to Johnson, this being chassis 60551, and Barker was appointed to build a four-seater touring body in the style known as the 'Roi-des-Belges'. Claude Johnson is recognized as having had particularly lavish taste when it came to motor cars, and in any case was noted for his general extravagance. His demands to Barker were that the coachwork be finished in aluminium paint, and that the exterior and interior fittings, to include headlamps, wheel hubs, door handles and windscreen, be silver-plated. Even the grease cups were similarly treated. The finishing touch was the scuttle-mounted silver plaque bearing the name Silver Ghost.

There remains some controversy regarding chassis 60551, in that for many years Rolls-Royce referred to it as being the 13th 40/50hp chassis to have been built. To this day company documentation attests to this, although the most eminent Rolls-Royce historians now acknowledge it to be the twelfth chassis. The most probable reason for the debate is that the chassis allocated the number 60543 was never built.

As on previous occasions, Claude Johnson anticipated that for maximum publicity the Silver Ghost should endure the most ardent testing. Experience with the car had shown it to be both robust and completely smooth in performance, and it was with every confidence that Johnson entered the 1907 Scottish Reliability Trials, which were held during the summer. Earlier in the year the car was greeted with huge acclaim when it was presented to the media: *The Autocar* commented that the vehicle was the smoothest running of any thus far tested, and likened the engine to a silent sewing machine. Praise indeed! One particular test that Claude Johnson performed was to place three tumblers on the bonnet, each filled with coloured water. The engine was then started and allowed to run at 1,150rpm while the event was photographed using a camera and film with a four-minute exposure. That picture testifies to the engine's lack of vibration, for not only was not a drop of water spilled, the resulting picture showed there to be a sharp outline of the tumblers.

Before the Scottish Reliability Trials proper, Claude Johnson undertook a 2,000-mile run using the Silver Ghost in competition with another vehicle, a 30hp White steamer driven by Frederick Coleman. Competition was hardly the name of the game however; the event was intended as nothing more than a friendly affair to ascertain the characteristics of both machines under arduous

The Silver Ghost with Claude Johnson at the wheel and C.S. Rolls seated at the rear nearest the camera. When this photograph was taken in 1907, Rolls-Royce had implemented a one-model policy and was preparing to move from Cooke Street to Derby. (Courtesy Rolls-Royce & Bentley Motor Cars Ltd)

conditions. The run was observed by the RAC, and the course included that which the Scottish Reliability Trials would cover. During the run the Silver Ghost with Claude Johnson at the wheel performed impeccably, there being an involuntary stop of a mere 40 seconds because of a lack of petrol pressure.

Having proved that the Silver Ghost was indeed a very fine motor car, Claude Johnson decided on a more arduous enterprise. Endurance testing was popular among some of the more prestigious vehicle makers at the time, and trials involving impressive distances had been conducted by the Siddeley and Hotchkiss marques. Claude Johnson's plan was to enter the Silver Ghost for the Scottish Reliability Trials, then continue running between London and Glasgow for a total of 15,000 miles.

Evidence shows that distances well in excess of that which Claude Johnson envisaged had been proposed by other marques, and the fact that RAC observers would have to endure the trauma of shuttling up and down the country week after week in what were not always the most comfortable or reliable of vehicles was an issue the club had debated. A limit of 15,000 miles was therefore imposed on endurance testing observations, and whether or not Claude Johnson would have preferred a more extensive trial is open to conjecture. What is known is that Johnson set out to better the 7,089-mile record established by a Siddeley car, and the RAC limit offered sufficient potential.

Claude Johnson insisted that he took control of the Silver Ghost during the Scottish Reliability Trials in which the car suffered just one minor difficulty when, after 628 miles, the petrol tap was shaken into the closed position on a particularly rough highland track. This was the only involuntary stop, the problem taking less than a minute to diagnose and rectify. After 4,000 miles at the wheel, Claude Johnson delegated the driving to C.S. Rolls, Reg Macready and Eric Platford, who completed the trial without further incident. What made the event all the more remarkable is that towards the later stages of the trials, members of the press were given, to their delight, the opportunity of following the Silver Ghost aboard another 40/50hp. This was another example of Claude Johnson's marketing and publicity prowess, as was his insistence that the RAC strip the Silver Ghost to examine every part, replacing those which showed signs of wear. Johnson's confidence in the vehicle and Rolls-Royce engineering did not let him down; an insignificant amount of wear was found in the steering assembly, the engine valves needed to be ground in, and repacking of the water pump was found necessary. In all, this was of little consequence bearing in mind the demanding circumstances of the trial, and the cost of repairs amounted to £2 2s 7d. To put this in its proper context, under normal driving conditions, the same mileage would have resulted in no work or expenditure being necessary.

The successful completion of the trials led to there being a welcome demand for the Silver Ghost by those motorists in the fortunate position of being able to afford such a prestigious motor car. Some 50 chassis were laid down at the factory, heralding a production span of some 18 years, during which time 6,173 cars were built. There were many coachwork styles produced by various bespoke coachbuilders, some better known than others, and invariably, because of the Silver Ghost's fame, a number were built in the Roi-des-Belges fashion.

Claude Johnson's one-model policy was seen to be the saviour of Rolls-Royce in a number of respects. Not only could production of the 40/50hp be finely tuned so that all the resources of the company could be channelled to make this the finest car it had yet offered, the building of the Derby factory had left the firm with minimal financial reserves, which prohibited any investment for producing alternative models.

Several occurrences following the opening of the Derby factory ultimately affected the company's future. Claude Johnson, ever seeking the best publicity, decided that by establishing the company's own driving school, optimum training for chauffeurs would prove entirely fruitful. Chauffeurs usually had an influence on the car the owner purchased, and if a Rolls-Royce was favoured by the chauffeur...

When it was decided that Royce should experiment with getting more power from the 40/50hp engine, two trials cars were built, one of which was entered in the 1908 Scottish Reliability Trials. This was chassis 60726, known as White Ghost but later renamed White Knave. The other was constructed for the International Touring Car Trial, also of 1908, this being chassis 60737, referred to as Silver Silence and renamed Silver Rogue. Both cars featured 70hp engines with mechanically operated overhead inlet valves, but the former car was withdrawn from the event after a piston seized. As for the latter vehicle, that was driven to its class victory with Eric Platford at the wheel, and was displayed at the opening ceremony of the Nightingale Road factory.

Built to compete in the 1908 International Touring Car Trial, this is chassis 60737, otherwise known as Silver Rogue. The car had an experimental 70hp engine with horizontal sparking plugs and exposed inlet valves. The plate K-86 is significant in that the car took first place in K class of the 1908 2,000-mile RAC trial with Eric Platford at the wheel. 1908 was, of course, the year that Rolls-Royce moved to Nightingale Road, Derby, from Manchester. (Courtesy Rolls-Royce & Bentley Motor Cars Ltd)

Rolls the Aviator

By the time the Silver Ghost had been successfully launched and the virtues of the 40/50hp had been demonstrated to the world, C.S. Rolls had involved himself in aviation in addition to motoring. At the turn of the century ballooning was establishing itself as a fashionable sport, but to participate one had to be wealthy. Rolls's background gave him that facility, and, just as he had once favoured pioneering French motor cars, he turned to that country for inspiration in ballooning. When Rolls became associated with a small

outfit of balloonists from Battersea in London, it was not long before they were being promoted to the front line of the sport. The alliance between Rolls and the Short brothers is well documented, and in retrospect the Shorts enjoyed an enviable position in the history of aviation. Rolls could always be relied upon to be at the forefront of ballooning events of any significance, and it was not long before he began to consider combining aviation with the internal combustion engine.

Rolls would have known that possibly the first 'dirigible' had made its maiden flight in 1883 when Gaston Tissandier piloted his steerable balloon courtesy of a Siemens electric motor. A year later *La France*, the world's first fully controllable airship, powered by a 9hp electric motor, took to the skies above the French town of Chalais-Meudon. Rolls took his first flight in a dirigible in 1908 at the invitation of Monsieur H.D. de la Meurthe; travelling to Paris, Rolls joined the crew of the airship *Ville de Paris* for what was to be his 100th ascent, an occasion which, according to the *London Magazine*, he enjoyed immensely. However, Rolls had by no means thought of abandoning ballooning. On the contrary, he relished the sport and, being one of the three founders of the Royal Aero Club, continued competing.

From ballooning Rolls moved on to powered flight. Since before going to Eton the young Rolls would have been aware of the heroic attempts of Sir Hiram Stevens Maxim (of Maxim machine-gun fame) and Clément Ader to become airborne with heavier-than-air machines, and in the ensuing years he followed the trials and tribulations of such pioneers as Louis Blériot and Gabriel Voisin, among others. There is evidence that Rolls was highly impressed by the exploits of the American Wright brothers at Kitty Hawk, especially Wilbur's

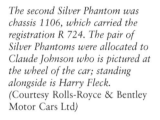

The second Silver Phantom was chassis 1106, which carried the registration R 724. The pair of Silver Phantoms were allocated to Claude Johnson who is pictured at the wheel of the car; standing alongside is Harry Fleck.
(Courtesy Rolls-Royce & Bentley Motor Cars Ltd)

false start ahead of Orville's first powered flight in December 1903. Instead of electricity or steam, it was a small petrol engine, designed and built by the Wrights' trusty engineer Charley Taylor, that provided the impetus. The Wright brothers subsequently made longer journeys and flew to ever higher altitudes to the amaze- ment of the spectators

C.S. Rolls used this car with its Victoria de luxe style of coachwork by H.J. Mulliner, chassis 60785, to transport his ballooning equipment. A similar car was also used by Rolls (chassis 60707), which became known as 'The Cookie'. (Courtesy Rolls-Royce & Bentley Motor Cars Ltd)

on the ground. Ultimately it was France where the brothers sought the manufacture of the Flyer, but it was Eustace Short that arranged to build six machines at his Shellbeach factory on the Isle of Sheppey in England. That was in 1908, and as far as the general public were concerned, flying had become acceptable.

On 8 October 1908 Rolls, who was visiting France at the same time as the Wright brothers, was invited to fly with Wilbur Wright. The event was succinctly documented in *Flight*, and Rolls was clearly captivated by the experience. Following his ascent he wrote: 'The sensation of flight was novel and delightful and the fact of accomplishing what several eminent scientists have "proved" impossible gave an added satisfaction.'

Rolls's association with the Short brothers meant that he would have known of the contract they had secured, and, given his interest in flying, it comes as little surprise to discover that the first machine to emerge from Shellbeach had in fact been ordered by Rolls. In truth Rolls was torn between his love of the motor car and his admiration of the flying machine, and for some time he succeeded in promoting both.

Now the owner of a Short biplane, Rolls's competitive spirit surfaced once again. Several attempts had been made at crossing the English Channel, and it was the achievement of a double crossing that Rolls pursued. Leaving from Dover on 2 June 1910 – there had been a couple of earlier false starts – Rolls successfully navigated towards Sangatte on the French coast, flew across that part of France and dropped a message of greeting to the Aero Club de France before setting course for Dover, where he was met by a huge and enthusiastic gathering.

With the advent of air shows around the country, the growing interest in flying was catered for by a select and daring group of aviators of which C.S. Rolls was one. Aerodromes, then known as flying fields, were inaugurated in France and thereafter were soon established in Britain, firstly at the Isle of Sheppey and then Brooklands. Air shows, otherwise known as flying meetings, were held at Doncaster and Blackpool, both events being somewhat curtailed

This elegant 40/50hp was owned by George Clark of the Saxone Shoe Company when this picture was taken in around 1912. Chassis 1929 carries coachwork by Dick Bros of Kilmarnock, one of a number of smaller coachbuilders specialising in individual commissions. The photograph gives a good indication of a chauffeur's uniform of the period. (Sir Henry Royce Memorial Foundation)

because of inclement weather. Mention has already been made of Massac Buist, and it was he who accompanied Rolls on a tour of the French airfields in a Silver Ghost. The tour was naturally very successful in publicising Rolls-Royce. It was also the Silver Ghost that was centre stage when the Wright brothers visited Britain, and Rolls escorted them when visiting the Short brothers at the Isle of Sheppey. Rolls served as ambassador to other international flyers, and entertained Blériot among others. He was also the second aviator to receive the Royal Aero Club's pilots' certificate on 8 March 1910 – the first had been J.T.C. Moore-Brabazon (later Lord Brabazon of Tara) – and the same year he is recorded as being the owner of as many as three aeroplanes.

Evidence exists that Rolls was contemplating the establishment of his own aeroplane manufacturing, possibly along similar lines as his motor car interests. A Rolls biplane is mentioned in 1909, although the machine was, at that time, still at the design stage. According to *Jane's All The World's Airships*, Gabriel Voisin was in discussion with Rolls, and had incorporated a number of his ideas into the proposed machine. Voisin makes no mention of his encounter with Rolls in his autobiography, and it can only be presumed that development ceased on Rolls's death.

The fact that Rolls was contemplating deeper involvement with the aircraft industry gives rise to speculation that his association with Henry Royce and Claude Johnson (and Rolls-Royce) was being tested. It would be totally incorrect to suggest that Rolls intended to detach himself from the Rolls-Royce marque, but it is known that his visits to Conduit Street became so irregular that his absence gave cause for concern to his two business partners. In his biography of Rolls, Lord Montagu of Beaulieu makes the point that Rolls would have to decide whether to remain Rolls-Royce's technical director, and therefore pursue flying as a hobby, or to become a full-time aviator and thus relinquish his appointment. From the writings of his contemporaries it seems clear that flying did govern Rolls's life, and this is substantiated by the fact that in January 1910 he asked his fellow Rolls-Royce directors whether they would consent to his surrendering some of his responsibilities because of other pressures, although he wished to remain on the board.

The board agreed to Rolls's request, and after that date there are few references concerning him and matters regarding Rolls-Royce. Once an ardent campaigner for the vehicles bearing his name, Rolls decided to delegate competing and demonstrating Rolls-Royce motor cars to others.

According to the biography of Claude Johnson, Rolls's surrendering of duties was more sinister, and heralded by an argument with Ernest Claremont. Despite Lillie Hall, once the premises of C.S. Rolls & Co., having been incorporated into the new company, Rolls nevertheless considered that he had ultimate control over its affairs. Claremont, taking a strict financial interest in Rolls-Royce as a whole, thought otherwise, especially when it was discovered that the premises were being used for the manufacture of a driveshaft assembly for an airship belonging to one of Rolls's friends instead of undertaking more profitable commercial automotive work. Rolls-Royce directors made an issue of

This undated photograph shows an unidentified 40/50hp but is nevertheless evocative. The build quality of the Silver Ghost made it an ideal vehicle for the type of terrain depicted. (Courtesy Mark Morris, Autovisage, and the Sir Henry Royce Memorial Foundation)

the matter; an argument developed, it is claimed, and Rolls, having been noted as a bad loser, from then on took a diminished interest in the company.

The forgoing illustrates Rolls's pragmatic approach to aviation. It can be supposed that Rolls tried in vain to persuade Henry Royce and Claude Johnson of the potential of powered flight. Royce appears to have doubted that aviation offered prosperity or serious enterprise, and even the usually opportunistic Claude Johnson appeared uncharacteristically impervious to its offers of future opportunities. It is probable that Rolls envisaged Rolls-Royce building aero-engines, but essentially Royce was far too busy with other matters, and he would have refused to construct anything that he had not designed himself. Had Rolls not met a premature death, the history of Rolls-Royce, the Derby factory, and indeed aviation and aero-engine technology, might have been rather different.

In other areas there was some recognition of the commercial aspects of flying, and with it evolved an acknowledgement that the aeroplane and airship had military potential. It was about the time of Rolls's diminishing interest in motor cars that he was approached by the War Office to assist in the training of pilots in the event of them being required for armed service. As it happened, the exercise was curtailed.

Even if Rolls's immediate contemporaries had little faith in the future of aviation, the government of the day did. There was support for the balloon factory at Farnborough, and in the wake of Rolls's double Channel crossing the same establishment incorporated aeroplanes in its interests in the form of the Air Battalion, which in 1913 was renamed the Royal Flying Corps. The RFC eventually grew into the RAF.

Rolls is Killed

In July 1910 Rolls was billed as the main attraction at Bournemouth, a flying event that was quite the most elaborate and extensive at the time. The air show, held at Southbourne on land which had been specially prepared, formed what were hailed as Bournemouth's centenary celebrations, and as well as aerial displays there were a host of proceedings ranging from motoring extravaganzas to a parade of two thousand Boy Scouts. Included in the programme of events

The reverse of this photograph bears the date 1913 and the picture shows the Nightingale Road factory in a deserted state. What would have been a highly emotive image is marred by the fact that it is lifeless, missing that one important element, people. This is a view of number one shop, its dimensions apparent only by the number of vehicles on the assembly lines. Clearly evident is the network of trolley rails connecting the shop with other areas of the factory. The movement of specially designed trucks around the works was introduced by Henry Royce in order to establish a measure of automation and efficiency. (Sir Henry Royce Memorial Foundation)

were concerts conducted by the most eminent conductors and composers of the day and, naturally, a series of sparkling social gatherings. Rolls was rightly honoured, for he, along with other pioneer aviators, had helped forge a whole new industry and science. Now recognized for his ground-breaking efforts in motoring, his name was also at the forefront of flying.

Among the competitive events at the Bournemouth display was a landing exercise, something which the self-taught Rolls confidently entered. The procedure was to take off, complete a circuit of the airfield and land, bringing the aircraft within a marked area. Rolls arrived at Bournemouth with his French-built Wright machine, which he had modified to include an additional rear outrigger, the design being intended to surround the existing outrigger in order to afford greater stability. Rolls had experienced a measure of difficulty with the arrangement and had decided to fit an additional elevator, thus dispensing with a fixed tailplane. In the event the elevator did not arrive until five days before the start of the airshow, and it was a further three days before it was fitted, which gave insufficient time for the aircraft to be properly tested.

The fact that Rolls's Wright biplane was largely unprepared did not prevent the flyer from participating in the first day's events on Monday 11 July. Rolls was, in fairness, a perfectionist, and would not have risked his neck had he considered his machine not to be airworthy. Although he attempted to better the altitude contest to establish a new British record, he did not succeed, although he did put on a distinguished display to the delight of his audience.

On Tuesday 12 July, the second day of the event, Rolls had entered the landing contest which, by nature of the layout of the landing area, was causing difficulty for the other pilots. The landing area, 100 yards in diameter with a

At the outbreak of war in 1914 motor manufacturing at Derby ceased except for the production of vehicles for war effort and a number of armoured vehicles such as the type depicted here. This is a standard Admiralty 1914-pattern Mark 1 armoured car, as supplied by Vickers from their depot at Erith in Kent. Vehicles such as this provided exemplary service throughout the war in the most hostile of conditions. (Courtesy Rolls-Royce & Bentley Motor Cars Ltd)

white marker at its centre, was positioned no more than 60 yards from the judging position, and the same distance from the grandstand. Witness accounts provide the clue that Rolls was not entirely happy that the velocity of the wind, which, together with the marker not being adequately distinct from the air, caused him to be pessimistic. Other aviators had similar misgivings, and when Rolls prepared himself for take-off at around 11.00am, he was beseeched by his fellow aviator Edmond Audemars to delay his flight until later in the day. Rolls, however, would not hear of changing his plans.

On his first attempt at alighting, Rolls had chosen a cross-wind approach, which had not been successful. He had two further attempts available to him, and on the first of these he decided to meet the wind head-on and to touch down with the nose of the craft pointing towards the grandstand.

Until beginning his descent everything had gone well, and Rolls had achieved a near-perfect manoeuvre. As he aimed to land precisely in the marker zone there was a loud snap from Rolls's aeroplane, part of the tail plane gave way, and the craft dropped like a stone to the earth. The machine was wrecked. Rolls was thrown clear but suffered chronic concussion. His death was virtually instantaneous.

Rolls was killed in a flying accident near Bournemouth on 12 July 1910. The tangled wreckage of his aeroplane can be seen. (Courtesy Sir Henry Royce Memorial Foundation)

Throughout the years there have been numerous suppositions and expert opinions about the actual cause of the aeroplane's failure and whether it was mechanical or a pilot error. Least said is best other than to state that the aviation and motor industries lost one their finest personalities and were thus all the poorer. Aged only 32 when he was killed, Rolls had packed more into his short life than most achieve in a full natural life span. He was buried in the churchyard at Rockfield near to the family home at The Hendre, and in Monmouth a monument was erected to the memory of the pioneer aviator and motorist. Rolls's contribution to air travel is also recorded at Dover, near to where he landed following his double crossing of the English Channel.

Royce and Ill-Health

Rolls's death was a severe blow to Henry Royce and Claude Johnson, and for the former the news aggravated his already delicate health. A workload beyond all reason as well as preparing the Derby factory eventually took its toll, and Royce was near to collapse. Despite his doctor's earlier advice, Royce had taken little heed and maintained a routine and pressure of work that few others could sustain.

Royce's illness was to put a severe strain on Claude Johnson who, as well as marketing Rolls-Royce motor cars, had taken over the sales side of the company when Rolls had asked to be relieved of some of his duties. For the 800 personnel working at Nightingale Road in 1911 the introduction of the Silver Ghost and the 40/50hp cars had proved a difficult passage, and continual development remained necessary, especially with rival manufacturers, namely Napier, Daimler and Lanchester, all vying for 'Carriage Folk' customers. The inauguration of the Chauffeur Driving School at Derby had been a brilliant initiative, and now Claude Johnson's foremost aim was to break into the market primarily enjoyed by Daimler, supplying motor cars to royalty and heads of state. The Royal Warrant was nevertheless retained by Daimler until 1959-60.

The 40/50hp was viewed by Rolls-Royce's rivals to be their main challenger. The smoothness of running and the engine's quietness was something that none of the competitors' cars could then match. It was only when Daimler, in an effort to produce a commensurately fine running vehicle, adopted the American Knight sleeve-valve engine, otherwise known as the Silent Knight, that any came close. The whole matter regarding the design principles of the engine gave rise to much controversy during the early 1900s, and it was acknowledged that while the engine had distinct advantages over other designs, there were some disadvantages. Quiet and smooth running the Knight engine certainly was, and it also displayed longevity; lubrication was a problem, however, and oil consumption was notably heavy. Several other respected car makers also chose to embrace sleeve-valve engines, but this did not prevent Claude Johnson from embarking on a personal campaign against Daimler. He even went so far as to acquire a 38hp model in order to compare it with the 40/50hp.

Ernest Hives and the Experimental Department

The question of testing and evaluating Rolls-Royce motor cars necessitates some explanation of the role in the company performed by Ernest Hives who, in 1937, was appointed general works manager. Born in 1886, it was Hives, along with Claude Johnson, who achieved so much in making Rolls-Royce the

'...in his memoirs he recounted stepping out of Derby railway station in the rain and, looking along Midland Road, being so depressed that he almost departed.'

company it now is. An accomplished motorist by the age of 14, Hives went to the assistance of a fellow driver repairing his car. That motorist was none other than C.S. Rolls, and their encounter led to the young Hives being engaged to work at Lillie Hall, firstly as a chauffeur-mechanic, and later as chief salesman at the Fulham premises. Having left Rolls's employment to take up an appointment with Owens before going to Napier at nearby Acton, Hives eventually joined Rolls-Royce at Derby in 1908. It was only by the toss of a coin that Hives did arrive at Nightingale Road: in his memoirs he recounted stepping out of Derby railway station in the rain and, looking along Midland Road, being so depressed that he almost departed. Ultimately he flipped a penny, which decided whether he would turn tail for home or continue on to Rolls-Royce...

It was Tom Haldenby to whom Ernest Hives reported that morning in 1908. Royce and Claude Johnson had acknowledged that a policy of continual improvement was a necessity, and therefore a fledgling experimental department was established at a time when the Nightingale Road workforce numbered no more than 400. Haldenby was in charge, and Hives, already a competent tester, was to be his assistant. While working for Napier, Hives had entered the 1907/1908 Scottish Reliability Trials, and there is evidence that he drove at Brooklands.

Work in the experimental department was varied, and testing was conducted on several cars. Of particular importance at the time was chassis 1701, which bore the registration number R 1075 and carried a lightweight touring body. Napier had somewhat stolen publicity from Rolls-Royce by undertaking an observed run between London and Edinburgh with the car's gearbox locked in top gear so as to publicise its flexibility and economy. Claude Johnson, unable to let such a feat pass by unchallenged, ordered 1701 to be tested accordingly. Trials were made using a higher compression ratio, an enlarged carburettor and completely revised rear suspension utilising cantilever springs and rear axle. Hives was entrusted with the preliminary road testing and undertook the London to Edinburgh course with good results. When under RAC observation, Hives completed the journey recording better than 24mpg, together with a measured top speed of 78mph. Known affectionately as 'the Sluggard', 1701, again with Hives at the wheel, was tested at Brooklands. The touring body replaced by a streamlined racing affair, Hives pushed 1701 through 100mph to attain a recorded top speed of 101mph.

Rolls-Royce customers learning of 1701's achievements were naturally keen to acquire a 40/50hp with the revised chassis arrangement, and as such the design was referred to as the 'London to Edinburgh'. Rolls-Royce offered the chassis as an alternative to the catalogue 40/50hp, and by 1914 it was standardised.

Experimental work was frequently tedious and often meant having to endure driving in bad weather with little or no protection. In those days motor cars were usually equipped with acetylene lighting, which was often at the mercy of the gas generator and, in any event, lacked the powerful illumination of modern vehicles. On this very point it was suggested by Lord Northcliffe that Rolls-Royce consider developing electric lighting and make it a standard feature on all new cars. Peculiarly for Claude Johnson he failed to accept the merit of the submission, replying that it would be too costly to install at a time when the company was concentrating its efforts in opening new markets in Europe.

It was an event in Europe that in 1912 rocked the very foundations of Rolls-Royce. The success of the Silver Ghost and subsequent accolades had allowed a degree of complacency to exist at Derby, and when it was noted that a 40/50hp that had been privately entered in the Austrian Alpine Trials had failed somewhat spectacularly, that confidence was shaken. When James Radley's car had baulked at the task of conquering the renowned Katschberg Pass because it was too highly geared, panic set in at Nightingale Road. The fact that Radley, a renowned pilot and motorist, who was first on the scene when Rolls crashed his aircraft at Bournemouth, managed to restart his car once two of his passengers had alighted was of little consolation.

Fully armoured 40/50hp vehicles were supplied at the request of the Indian government for peace-keeping purposes. The chassis were delivered to Vickers, who designed and built the armour; above the turret is the commander's cupola which could revolve and therefore provided both an observation point as well as some additional security. (Courtesy Rolls-Royce & Bentley Motor Cars Ltd)

One of the reasons for the Austrian misfortune was that despite Rolls-Royce's determination to become a powerful competitor in the European market, little, if any, testing had been conducted there. The testing grounds of Derbyshire, the Lake District and Scotland were thought to be sufficient. If Rolls-Royce was to compete effectively with its European rivals, changes were needed.

Eric Platford and Ernest Hives were put in charge of examining every aspect of the 40/50hp, and given responsibility for preparing three cars that would be entered into the following year's Austrian Alpine Trials. Platford was despatched to Austria where he experienced the arduous driving conditions first hand. Hives, recognising that time was of the essence, installed at Nightingale Road an ingenious device that could subject a chassis to the rigours of months of gruelling use in mere days. The chassis bump rig therefore became an essential and integral feature of the newly-established experimental department, which then comprised some five technicians.

The results of the bump rig were instrumental in highlighting the need for a number of necessary modifications to the 40/50hp chassis. Royce chose to develop cantilever rear suspension and, contrary to previous policies regarding transmission systems, adopted a four-speed gearbox as a substitute for the previously favoured three-speed affair. Further revisions to the chassis design included provision of greater ground clearance and a radiator with increased capacity, along with a larger block and header tank. The modifications were sufficient for Rolls-Royce to bestow the title of 'Continental' on the chassis.

The 1913 Austrian Alpine Trials thus saw four Rolls-Royce entrants. The Derby factory team comprised three cars, driven by Hives, Friese and Sinclair, and James Radley, the owner of Portholme coachbuilders, was again a private entry. The Rolls-Royce Continentals swept the board and the company was once again victorious. As for the Continentals, further modifications ensued; the models were fitted with electric lighting and starting, together with a new braking system. It was not long before the models were unofficially referred to as 'Alpine Eagles'. That was in 1914, the year World War One broke out.

James Radley – he was known as Jimmy – was one of a number of Rolls-

Royce owners who, with their cars, were drafted into military service during World War One. It was once the horse that was the prime means of transport in war, but now the internal combustion engine took on that role. The Royal Automobile Club Corps was formed in the summer of 1914 when a band of motorists offered their services by volunteering to convey military personnel wherever and whenever required. Some of those volunteers, like the Duke of Westminster, were Rolls-Royce owners, and their efforts are now recognised as being particularly courageous under the most dangerous of conditions. Rolls-Royce motor cars saw service at the very heart of hostilities, and were used for a wide variety of purposes including ambulances.

Rolls-Royce Armoured Cars

For transporting of generals and the like, the Silver Ghost in war is probably best remembered as an armoured car. It was the Belgians who first appreciated the potential the motor vehicle offered as a fighting vehicle, even if such machines were nothing more than cars stripped of their coachwork and fitted with improvised bodies produced in railway workshops. Winston Churchill was an early advocate of using converted motor cars as support vehicles for air squadrons, and when a fleet was sent to France and Belgium during the early stages of the war they caused havoc among the enemy. Under the direction of Commander Samson RN, as much good use as possible was made of the vehicles, and often they were fitted with better protection than had originally been provided.

In October 1914 the Royal Naval Armoured Car Division came into being under the command of Commander F.L. Boothby RN. It was apparent that only the finest types of vehicle were capable of supporting the armour and weaponry necessary for such a task, and it was Rolls-Royce that the military approached to supply a number of suitable machines. Rolls-Royce also provided many of the skilled mechanics that were required to keep the armoured cars in optimum condition. The support crews were mostly recruited from the Nightingale Road factory, and it was the men who had the most experience that were despatched to the fighting front. In December 1914 the first batch of armoured cars was delivered to No.1 Squadron of the RNAC Division. Comprising a dozen vehicles, the squadron was sent to the East Anglia coast on exercise, should the enemy attempt a landing. It was a remarkable feat that the squadron, with its vehicles each weighing nearly four tons, could maintain speeds in excess of 40mph. The Rolls-Royces provided exemplary service, although the uprated suspension designed for them was insufficient, and modifications were undertaken. Stronger springs were fitted, following locomotive practice, and subsequently all vehicles were so produced without there being any further problems.

Deliveries of vehicles proceeded at a rapid rate, 12 divisions being furnished by the end of January 1915. Difficulties were experienced in equipping the vehicles with the specified armaments, thus a number were fitted with Maxims supplied from naval fleets. No.2 Squadron, with its complement of 12 Rolls-Royces, three heavily armoured lorries and a detachment of support vehicles, was the first to see action in France; Nos 3 and 4 Squadrons were detailed to Gallipoli before being sent to Egypt to defend the Suez Canal, and No.1

Squadron was drafted to German south-west Africa. The service record of the cars was beyond doubt, and they were described as being 'simply priceless'; when a detachment of vehicles was sent to Nairobi for refit, they afterwards continued with supreme reliability. Rolls-Royce publicity material is explicit in detailing the operational achievement of these cars in creating a probable record for the whole of the war: actively engaged in the most arduous campaigning for a full two years before being handed over to the army in Egypt, they had not given any trouble due to defects of materials or design.

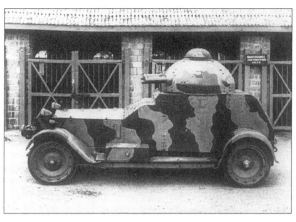

Pictured at Vickers' Erith works, this 40/50hp armoured car has two Vickers guns as well as camouflage which appears to be effective. From the time the chassis was delivered, it usually took four months to complete the vehicle. (Sir Henry Royce Memorial Foundation and Eric Barras)

Armoured car divisions were relinquished by the navy in favour of the army in 1915, at which time many of the vehicles were converted to staff cars. When General Sir H. Smith-Dorien was appointed to command the East African force he was quick to acknowledge the outstanding record of the armoured car divisions and utilised them for expeditionary use. The vehicles were subjected to laborious work in East Africa, the terrain being particularly difficult. Locating traps and anti-bear holes were common occurrences for Rolls-Royce drivers, and it was not unknown for vehicles to be overturned because of the conditions. Seldom was it the case that the vehicles were off the road for more than a few hours while being repaired, and even accounting for the tactics of the enemy, the armour of the Silver Ghosts always withstood the harshest treatment.

The role of the Silver Ghost during World War One has been recorded elsewhere, and it is sufficient to mention that the vehicles saw action in a number of theatres including Europe, Russia, the Balkans, Romania and Alexandria. There were heroic instances in respect of those military personnel accompanying the cars, and there were many occasions where the cars themselves proved their worth beyond any doubt. To cite one vehicle which had endured over 53,000 miles campaigning, the items that required replacement amounted to nothing more than a pair of front springs and a front-wheel ball race.

Of all the exploits recorded regarding Rolls-Royce armoured cars, few can match those of T.E. Lawrence, or 'Lawrence of Arabia'. In *Seven Pillars of Wisdom*, Lawrence provides a graphic account of the work performed by the vehicles and their crews, and of the Silver Ghost he wrote 'A Rolls in the desert was above rubies'.

As well as providing motive power on the ground, Rolls-Royce was dominating the skies, and in this respect it was Royce, Hives, and the workforce at the Derby factory who were at the front line.

CHAPTER FOUR

EAGLES AND AERO-ENGINES

A YEAR AFTER Rolls's death Henry Royce collapsed, partly through overwork and self-neglect, but also because of recurring illness. His condition was so serious that doctors gave him, at most, three months to live. It would be under-stressing the point to say that the Derby personnel were in turmoil: without Royce at the helm it seemed an alien situation, and many thought that there was every chance of the company floundering. Claude Johnson rose to the challenge of not only maintaining business as usual, but also organising a tour of Europe and beyond for Royce, on the premise that a period of rest and travel might help him recuperate.

The fact that Royce left Derby, to return only once, is testament to the thorough way in which the company conducted itself. Despite his illness, Royce nevertheless remained firmly in charge of affairs, and his design teams followed wherever he ventured. Royce was operated on in Norwich in 1911, and it is said that he took little heed of his doctors' prognosis. Leaving hospital, Royce returned to Overstrand for a period of convalescence that was supervised by Nurse Ethel Aubin, who had been specially hired to look after him. Mention has already been made of Minnie Royce's unease regarding illness, which is why the temporary appointment of a trained nurse was necessary.

In August 1911 Claude Johnson arranged for Nurse Aubin and her charge to travel to France. They took the train from Norwich to London, and from there to Dover, where they crossed the English Channel and continued by train to Tours. Johnson was there to meet the couple with his 40/50hp, which he named 'The Charmer', and the party set off for Italy, where they embarked on a cruise to Egypt. The travels to warmer climes were as a result of following Royce's doctors' advice, and wintering there was a prelude to a stay at Le Canadel in southern France.

One of Royce's medical advisors was Dr H. Campbell-Thomson, a highly respected Harley Street neurologist who happened to be a Rolls-Royce customer. A friend of both Royce and Claude Johnson, Dr Campbell-Thomson

When Royce was taken seriously ill, Claude Johnson took him to his home, Villa Jaune, at Le Canadel on the French Riviera, to recuperate. Royce felt so much at ease there that he arranged to have a house built for himself nearby, Villa Mimosa, which he adopted as his winter residence. Within the complex were built Le Bureau (the design office) and Villa Rossignol, where the design staff resided. This photograph shows Villa Jaune (centre right) and below it Villa Mimosa. Immediately below Royce's villa is Le Bureau which is partially obscured by Villa Rossignol, and below that is the garage that incorporated the electrical generator which provided power to the complex. On the extreme left is the villa that was owned by the Michelin family, and extreme right can be seen Le Canadel's hotel. (Courtesy Sir Henry Royce Memorial Foundation)

became the medical consultant for Rolls-Royce Ltd. Among his duties he visited Nightingale Road every month to give each of the executive personnel a health check, a routine that he performed until 1940. It was Campbell-Thompson's influence that led to Claude Johnson implementing a staff pension scheme, which was a welcome addition to the employees' financial security.

It was to his villa on the Côte d'Azur that Claude Johnson took Royce and Nurse Aubin on their return from Egypt. It was there, amid the Mediterranean landscape and mild climate, that Royce felt completely comfortable. Working at Derby remained out of the question for him, and he decided that he would live, during the winter months at least, at Le Canadel. Without delay Johnson began building a villa for Royce in the vicinity of his own house, Villa Jaune. Royce was specific in his requirements: within easy reach of the villa he would have a design office, adjacent to which would be accommodation for those design personnel outposted from the Derby factory.

What transpired was the development of a colony associated with Royce and Rolls-Royce. Villa Mimosa, a quite magnificent edifice, was built to Royce and Claude Johnson's instructions a little way from Villa Jaune, itself a glorious mansion, and nearby was the design studio, Le Bureau, an equally impressive building. Within the complex another villa, Le Rossignol, provided comfortable living quarters for the designers. The fact that Royce was situated so far from the Derby factory obviously resulted in huge problems when it came to communicating between the two places. At least one matter was solved though: the distance did at least enable the thorough testing of motor vehicles. When Royce wished to try out a car, it had to be driven to the French Riviera.

Royce would spend the summer months in England, but sufficiently far away from Derby to prevent the harsh climate and industrial fumes from further impairing his health. Initially Royce chose to live at Crowborough in Sussex, but later moved to a house at St Margaret's Bay near Dover, a short distance from where Claude Johnson had another of his villas. A short stay at Bognor

Royce spent the summer months in England at West Wittering on the south coast near the Solent. This is Elmstead, the house that Royce purchased; once a farmhouse, the property incorporated some outbuildings that were used as a piggery, and it is there that the design staff were established in converted and completely refurbished accommodation. (Courtesy Sir Henry Royce Memorial Foundation)

Regis was followed by the purchase of a farmhouse at West Wittering in Sussex, and there Royce ultimately set up home in England. Adjacent to 'Elmstead' (Royce had changed the name of the West Wittering farmhouse from Elm Tree Farm), the piggery was converted to a workshop for Royce's benefit; buildings nearby were rehabilitated to serve as a studio where Derby designers worked, and were renamed 'Camacha'. It was about the time of the outbreak of war in 1914 that Henry Royce finally separated from his wife Minnie, and he set up home at Elmstead with Ethel Aubin. She remained Royce's constant companion, and there is no doubt that had it not been for her faithful care and loyal attention, Royce would not have survived a further 22 years. Royce continued to provide for Minnie until she died, but on his death he did leave a substantial part of his estate to Ethel Aubin, who was given charge of his ashes.

Claude Johnson Takes Charge

The period immediately after Royce's departure from Derby was one of much difficulty for Rolls-Royce's senior executives. On Royce's collapse Claude Johnson put into operation a system of command at Derby and Conduit Street, London. It was Lord Herbert Scott to whom Claude Johnson delegated the day-to-day-running of the company from Conduit Street, where he was ably assisted by William Cowen, who was eventually appointed sales manager. At Derby the management team comprised Arthur Wormald, who was appointed general works manager and who, consequently, was appointed to the board of directors; Tom Haldenby also played a significant role, having been appointed assistant general manager, and Eric Platford became chief tester. Johnson knew only too well that Platford would not allow any chassis to be despatched from Nightingale Road unless it was to the standard that Royce himself would have expected. Another person who was to later play a most important role in the business of Rolls-Royce was R.W. Harvey-Bailey, a brilliant engineer appointed by Claude Johnson to ensure that quality engineering was in safe and careful hands. Also at Rolls-Royce at the time were a number of other highly qualified engineers, namely A.G. Elliott, Ernest Hives, Arthur Rowledge and Arthur Sidgreaves, all of whom had been secured from Rolls-Royce's closest rival, Napier.

While Royce's departure from Derby had left an obvious void, it has been recorded that in some quarters his absence was marked with a measure of relief. Recognised as being a terror for work, Royce once kept going for some 60 hours without a break, even for nourishment, and the fact that he was able to maintain such a performance was little comfort to those with a lesser constitution. When factory personnel took longer to carry out a task than it

Ivan Evernden, seen here with Henry Royce, joined the company at Nightingale Road in 1916 having failed his medical on call-up for military service. Initially assigned to the drawing office, Evernden was appointed to the airship design office and it was while he was working there that Henry Royce noticed him. He was promoted to become one of Royce's design specialists, and despite an early career with airships he was mainly engaged on motor car work. After World War Two Evernden moved to Crewe as chief project engineer and retired in 1961. (Courtesy Sir Henry Royce Memorial Foundation)

would have taken Royce, or when in his opinion the end result did not meet his exacting standards (which was arguable in some cases) they risked instant dismissal.

Royce had made the rule that nothing but British-made tools be used at Derby, a directive that was not entirely appreciated until after the outbreak of war in 1914. When some other manufacturers who had installed foreign tooling were unable to locate the necessary equipment to keep them operating, Rolls-Royce did not experience those difficulties.

With Royce isolated from Derby, the line of communication between him, his designers and the factory personnel was tenuous to say the least. Nevertheless the system, which anywhere other than Rolls-Royce would surely have failed, did work, albeit with some complications from time to time. In order to relieve Royce of as much stress as possible it was essential that his designers could mostly anticipate his demands, and demonstrate a tolerant and enduring personality that would not antagonise him.

At their outposted quarters design engineers would interpret Royce's wishes by completing their schemes on tracing paper. The essential tool by the side of the drawing board was an india rubber, which would be used time and again to change even the slightest detail at Royce's command. In the interest of Royce's health, and no doubt to minimise the stress on the design team members, the number of personnel working directly with him was kept to a minimum. Only when Royce was completely satisfied with a design were the tracing paper drawings sent to Nightingale Road. It would be obvious from the state of the drawings and the patches of thinness on them the number of alterations Royce had demanded.

In the drawing office at Nightingale Road the original designs were transferred to blueprints and then returned to Royce and his designers. At that time blueprints were produced using a wet process, a disadvantage being that they shrank, thus posing difficulties when it was necessary for designers to make tracing copies. There was constant dialogue between the Derby drawing office and the design team, and what could easily have evolved into a problematic situation was delicately handled by R.W. Harvey-Bailey. Claude Johnson recognised Harvey-Bailey as an engineer of the highest repute, having began his career with Colonel Pennington at the Horseless Carriage Co., which was based at the Motor Mills in Coventry. Both the Horseless Carriage Co. and the Motor Mills were very much part of Britain's fledgling motor industry.

Harvey-Bailey's assistant in the Derby drawing office was the highly capable Bill Clough, who headed a team of four section supervisors, one being responsible for engines, another frames, and the remaining two concerning themselves with gears and electrical aspects. Very much associated with the drawing office and the design team was the experimental department, where Ernest Hives did much of the day-to-day running.

While Royce was combating illness a major fight was developing in the Rolls-Royce board room. Sir Max Aitken, the Canadian newspaper magnate who later was better known as Lord Beaverbrook, instrumented a take over of Rolls-Royce with plans to re-register the firm in Canada. The business dealings were acrimonious, and finally Aitken withdrew his scheme, selling his substantial holding of Rolls-Royce shares to the American tycoon J.B. Duke. Duke was a Rolls-Royce customer, and when the end of the war was in sight, he was courted by Claude Johnson as a possible partner in the manufacture of Rolls-Royce aero-engines in the USA.

War – Rolls-Royce to the Rescue

At the outbreak of war in 1914 Rolls-Royce faced possibly its greatest challenge. The company was thrust into a state of crisis that could have resulted in it going into liquidation. Not only did the uncertainty of war have a devastating effect on the sale of motor cars, but the Rolls-Royce board's reluctance to involve the company with aero-engine manufacturing could also have cost Rolls-Royce, its shareholders, customers, personnel and, not least, the country, dearly.

In a number of respects Britain had largely ignored the military aspects of air power, but there were at least some visionaries that had the foresight to accept that the aeroplane offered the armed forces a powerful weapon of combat. The aeroplane had already been used in conflict before the onslaught of World War One: when the Italians had fought the Turks in Libya in November 1911, bombs were dropped from aircraft in warfare for the first time.

Air power for military operations was seen by various governments as a huge leap forward in defence. When the Royal Flying Corps was established in 1912 with a mere 50 aeroplanes, France, by comparison, had an effective air force

comprising 200 aircraft. Elsewhere in Europe both Bulgaria and Turkey had their own dedicated air corps; further afield, Japan was operating a naval air service, and America was demonstrating how aeroplanes, having been launched from ships, could embark upon combat using onboard machine guns. Germany, which had previously been committed to the use of airships, also adopted the aeroplane as a means of defence, and in October 1912 established its Military Aviation Service, which was supported by 100 machines and several airships.

When Britain went to war in 1914 the aircraft at the country's disposal included the Royal Aircraft Factory's BE2c, a slow but nevertheless safe reconnaissance machine that pilots found unwieldy to fly. The Royal Naval Air Service additionally operated a number of Maurice Farman IIs and Henri Farman HF20s, along with the Short 184 Seaplane, Airco DH2, RE8, Avros, and Blériot monoplanes.

Before his death Rolls had encouraged Rolls-Royce to acquire the UK rights to manufacture the Wright aeroplane. This would have enabled the company to provide engines to power the aircraft, engines which Rolls considered more efficient than that originally fitted. Rolls's proposal was flatly rejected. Shortly before the outbreak of World War One, James Radley, who was noted for his success in the Austrian Alpine Trials, had asked Royce to supply a modified 40/50hp engine for airship and aircraft use. When Radley had visited Royce at St Margaret's Bay, they had watched an airship struggle to make progress against a strong headwind along the Kent coast, and despite Radley's assurances that a Rolls-Royce engine would provide the means of efficiently powering the craft, Royce continued to maintain his objection to designing and building aero-engines. There is, nevertheless some indication that Royce was inspired by Radley's enthusiasm, which ultimately helped to him to later reverse his decision.

When the German army invaded Belgium's frontier on Tuesday 4 August 1914, Britain was declared to be at war from midnight, following a refusal from Germany to withdraw its troops. The Rolls-Royce company was plunged into a desperate situation when an order was received from Conduit Street to immediately discharge half the design and technical personnel, and to drastically reduce the salaries of the remaining staff. Henry Royce was among the first to take a severe cut in salary, and those who came into contact with him reported his frugal lifestyle.

The gloomy prospect of Rolls-Royce going out of business was very real. Production of motor cars ceased because the market for luxury vehicles had completely evaporated, and the personnel that remained at Derby were put on short time. The company's wage bill was reduced to one quarter of what it had

As a company Rolls-Royce was reluctant to enter aero-engine production and did so because of government pressure in the interests of the war effort. The company's first aero-engine was the Eagle, which was designed by Henry Royce in collaboration with A.G. Elliott. Design work commenced in 1914 and within six months it was being tested. The Eagle was designed for 200hp but experience showed it could produce much more power. Of V12 configuration, the Eagle was water-cooled and had a capacity of 20.32 litres. At a time when many engineers favoured air for cooling, Royce believed that water cooling was more appropriate. The Eagle was fitted to a diversity of aircraft, not least the Vickers Vimy. (Courtesy Sir Henry Royce Memorial Foundation)

been. In his message to those Rolls-Royce employees who faced being discharged, Claude Johnson encouraged them to sign up at once and join the armed forces. Those remaining at Derby he advised not to pay any rent because of their decrease in pay, and assured them that should they be evicted from their homes, they could live in the factory. Despite these panic measures emerging from both Conduit Street and Nightingale Road, the company resolutely remained opposed to aero-engine manufacturing, and Claude Johnson took the unprecedented step of placing an advertisement in the *Daily Mail*. Company personnel were on holiday when they read in the newspaper that they were to return home without delay and demonstrate rigid economy measures. When Claude Johnson addressed personnel both at Derby and in London, he warned them that the company's bankers might well freeze Rolls-Royce's assets.

Few people during the late summer of 1914 could have perceived that the war would extend for such a long period. Propaganda had led folk to believe that troops would be home by Christmas, and therefore it is reasonable to suggest that the common feeling around the board room table at Conduit Street was that the company could ride out the storm, and that normality would be quickly resumed.

There were those at Derby who took the view that war presented a real threat to Rolls-Royce's existence. Arthur Biddulph, the night-shift superintendent, was one such visionary, and it was partly due to him that work continued building the 40/50hp chassis for armoured cars, staff cars and ambulances. Additionally work was secured building shell cases, along with torpedo components and a hand-held dart that was designed to be dropped from aeroplanes above enemy trenches. Known as flechettes, the darts were capable of piercing a soldier's helmet and killing him instantly.

The decision by the Rolls-Royce board not to undertake aero-engine work for the British government prompted Royce and Johnson to take independent action. The board had acted in Royce's absence, and Royce chose personally to ignore the ruling. In what presented itself as a desperate situation, Claude Johnson felt he could no longer abide by the board's decision and personally approached the War Office. When shareholders disapproved of his action they were merely reminded that without such work there would not be a company; Rolls-Royce, he reminded them, had an important part to play in the country's future.

The War Office, relieved to receive the Rolls-Royce offer of help, persuaded Claude Johnson to build under licence 50 Renault V8 aero-engines. The fact that the British Government relied heavily upon France is significant, for that country's lead in establishing air power had encouraged ministers to believe that in time of crisis the French would be able to provide the necessary equipment. In the event, when the British sought supplies from France they were not forthcoming. There were a number of reasons for this, including the fact that the French considered that their own needs had priority, and that in-fighting between the Admiralty and the War Office resulted in there not being a collective approach made to France. In essence, though, there is evidence that the French were not in a position to be provider for all.

Several months before the outbreak of war, the Royal Aircraft Factory at Farnborough had been commissioned to design and build an aero-engine, this being in response to the lack of any other suitable British aero-engines available. With the onslaught of hostilities Farnborough's engine was nowhere near ready, hence the need to buy from abroad.

Royce's agreement to build Renault engines was reached only after a number of conditions had been satisfied, and in these Claude Johnson played an important role. Accepting that Royce would not consent to the full-scale building of engines other than those of his own design, Johnson at least secured vital work for Derby. In so doing he paved the way for the Royal Aircraft Factory agreeing to Royce's demands. Mervyn O'Gorman conducted the negotiations on behalf of Farnborough; he had already perceived that it was a 200bhp air-cooled affair that was required, and accordingly asked both Napier and Rolls-Royce to build examples.

As for Royce capitulating on his earlier decision not to build aero-engines, several reasons for him doing so have at various times been suggested. Was it the fact that Rolls-Royce was so desperate for work? Did he eventually accept that aviation had a prominent role to play as a means of civil transport as well as military combat? Did Rolls's flying accident and his ultimate death inspire Royce sufficiently to consider the worthiness of air power? Or was it the fact that his own illness and subsequent move away from the factory permitted Royce to take a more reflective view towards advancing technology? There is probably no single or simple answer, apart from to say that a number of factors led Royce to adopt a more liberal policy towards aviation.

What is certain is that Royce was totally against building an air-cooled engine in conjunction with Napier. Royce favoured water-cooling, for it was liquid-cooled engines that he understood so well, and he considered that an air-cooled engine would take too long to develop and would be costly in terms of Rolls-Royce's resources. Mervyn O'Gorman, despite not sharing Royce's convictions, was hardly in a position to dispute with Royce, and consequently arranged for as much assistance as possible to be given to Rolls-Royce in order that the company might begin immediate development, while producing a limited number of Renault V8s.

Reviewing this particular period in Rolls-Royce history a precursor to later events is witnessed. The fact that Royce had no intention of working alongside Napier brings Commander Wilfred Briggs into the picture. Briggs's assistant was none other than Lieutenant Walter Owen (W.O.) Bentley who, in 1931, was in the process of selling his car-making business to Napier when Rolls-Royce successfully acquired the firm from under Napier's nose in somewhat controversial circumstances.

Commander Wilfred Briggs was assigned to provide as much support to Rolls-Royce as possible, and in so doing introduced to Royce and his design team the young engineer Roy Fedden, who had served an apprenticeship with the Bristol Motor Company before joining the Brazil Straker company at Fishponds near Bristol. During his early career with Brazil Straker, Fedden designed a small car, known as the Shamrock, that met with much acclaim. Again there is coincidence: Fedden went to public school at Clifton, where he

Shortly after designing the Eagle, the Derby aero-engine team devised a much smaller engine, which became known as the Hawk. A six-cylinder water-cooled and ungeared unit which initially developed 75hp, it was used to propel a number of airships. This photograph, dating from around 1916, depicts airships S.S.Z59 and S.S.Z60, the former aboard HMS Furious. Hawks were developed to provide more power and were fitted to a number of aircraft in addition to airships. (Courtesy Sir Henry Royce Memorial Foundation)

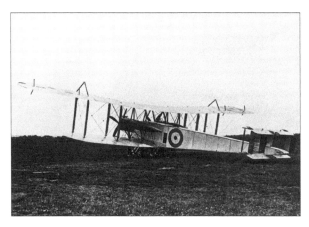

The first aeroplane to be fitted with the Eagle engine was the Handley Page 0/100 bomber. The inaugural flight was made from Hendon Aerodrome on 18 December 1915. Illustrated here is HP 0/100 1457. (Courtesy Royal Air Force Museum, ref. P6862)

met Bentley, who was younger; Fedden's father bought a motor car at about the same time as Royce, both having chosen a Decauville.

Before the outbreak of war Roy Fedden had visited Germany in an attempt to arrange with the Bosch company supplies of electrical equipment for the 1914 model year Straker Squire cars. When visiting Stuttgart, Fedden was taken by Bosch to the Mercedes factory, where he could watch Bosch equipment being fitted, and while there took the opportunity to wander around other areas of the factory. Quite unintentionally Fedden found himself in a large assembly workshop where rows of six-cylinder water-cooled engines were being built. It was at once obvious to Fedden that these were aero-engines, and he was concerned that Germany's air power posed a considerable threat to the Allies. There is little doubt that Fedden informed Briggs of his findings, for the two were well acquainted.

A Mercedes with an advanced design of engine had won the 1914 French Grand Prix, and after the event the car was brought to London, where it was put into storage in a car showroom in Shaftesbury Avenue. Briggs unearthed the car immediately following the outbreak of war and took it, along with Roy Fedden, to Rolls-Royce at Derby, where the engine was closely examined. Commander Briggs, having established that there was a requirement for 100, 150 and 200bhp aero-engines, and Royce having decided to develop a water-cooled version of the latter type, decided that Derby might be interested in seeing the Mercedes unit. What was found was an engine similar in design to that which Fedden had seen at Stuttgart. Despite Royce having been told to avoid the factory, he nevertheless travelled there on this occasion to examine the engine, the only such time he had done so since his illness; it was also his last visit.

The Mercedes engine was given to Arthur Wormald, who entrusted the running of it and its analysis to the experimental department under the watchful eye of Ernest Hives. Studying an engine in this manner was not something new, for Royce had instigated a policy of closely examining anything that was considered useful in respect of advancing technology. Rolls-Royce was not alone in doing this; other companies also made a point of investigating equipment for exploratory purposes. It is essential to emphasise that in no way did Rolls-Royce copy or attempt to copy the Mercedes engine: Royce had his own ideas about design and was as much interested in those as avoiding any Mercedes patents. The 40/50hp Silver Ghost engine provided the basis around which Royce designed his aero-engine, which he demanded should be a V12, having two banks of six cylinders arranged at an angle of 60 degrees.

The reason for Royce deciding upon a V12 was that it was not appropriate to increase the piston diameter of that used in the 40/50hp engine; it was possible, however, to increase the travel length of the piston from 4.75 inches to 6.5 inches. Overhead valves that were driven by an overhead camshaft were more suitable than the side valve arrangement inasmuch as they were more efficient in terms of providing power, although they were not so quiet in operation. The cast-iron cylinder blocks used on the Silver Ghost engine were discarded because of the weight factor, and in their place Royce chose to design pressed-steel water jackets to surround individual cylinders. Furthermore it was necessary to increase the engine speed to around 1,800rpm, which meant that a reduction gear was necessary if he were to achieve a propeller speed of under 1,100rpm, the figure advocated by the RNAS in the interest of maintaining propeller efficiency.

Royce chose a select design team to work with him at his home at St Margaret's Bay where he had spent most of the summer. It included A.G. Elliott, Royce's principal design assistant, who later became executive vice-chairman of Rolls-Royce, and Maurice Olley, a gifted engineer who achieved much for the company in both Britain and America before transferring to General Motors. Royce would normally have returned to Le Canadel for the winter period, but did not do so for two particular reasons. Not only did he want to remain in England to be as near the factory as possible while he wrestled with his aero-engine design, it was also decided, by Claude Johnson and Nurse Aubin, that to venture across the Channel at that time presented too great a risk.

Eagles Take to the Skies

In typical fashion Royce responded to the national emergency with indefatigable effort, working with A.G. Elliott and Maurice Olley from early morning until late evening, all the time calculating and producing drawings for the engine's 2,000 components. Exactly as Royce and his team had continually experimented with those early motor cars at Cooke Street, so he applied the same philosophy to aero-engines. 'There is no safe way of judging anything except by experiment' he repeatedly told his staff.

Royce's first aero-engine was the Eagle, and by February 1915 a prototype was on the test-bed at Derby. Royce's decision to enter aero-engine design and manufacturing called for the installation of suitable test facilities which, until the outbreak of war, did not exist at Nightingale Road. It was Ernest Hives who took responsibility for the design and installation of the test-beds, and in doing so called for the co-operation of the aviation industry's experts. In his biography of Ernest Hives, Alec Harvey-Bailey refers to that engineer's great flair in this respect, and his understanding of in-flight attitudes and the effect components had on them. Having taken six months from the emergence of the first drawings to reach the testing stage was nothing less than miraculous, especially since the designers and build team were separated by some 200 miles. There was frenetic communication between Kent and Derby: drawings would be rushed to Nightingale Road, where the components were made up, initially in wood, for Royce's examination. Only when he was entirely satisfied that the design was right – and there is evidence that certain components were taken to and fro from Derby several times – would he agree to the part being forged in its final state.

One particular aspect of the Eagle's construction that requires some explanation is the design of the pistons, which were forged in aluminium to minimise weight. Indeed weight was the critical factor throughout the engine's entire development. It was W.O. Bentley who was responsible, having experimented using aluminium pistons in his French DFP cars before the war. Bentley had once seen a souvenir paperweight forged in aluminium, and this

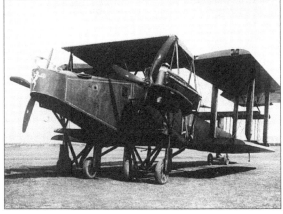

gave him the idea of improving an engine's performance while keeping it as lightweight as possible. His idea had worked, and Bentley went on to achieve some impressive motor-sport victories both on the race track and hill climb. Using aluminium pistons in aero-engines had occurred to him, and shortly after war had broken out, Bentley approached the Admiralty to further his idea. It was Commander Wilfred Briggs to whom Bentley was introduced, and before long both were meeting Ernest Hives at Derby. W.O. Bentley is also recognised as being a highly competent aero-engine designer, and as creator of his BR1 and BR2 rotary aero-engines contributed enormously to the war effort.

Nightingale Road had its own foundry, and components were made to the highest specification under the careful attention of Hives and his materials specialist, Buchanan. While Arthur Wormald was in overall charge at the factory, it was Claude Johnson who saw that all development was carried out as smoothly as possible, in accordance with the plethora of instructions that Royce dispatched from Kent. In his autobiography, Bentley mused that while at Nightingale Road, Hives took the sensible precaution of having W.O's calculations and material specifications carefully checked.

Putting the Eagle through its first test was a historic occasion. For those engineers and mechanics that for weeks had watched the machine steadily grow, anxiety reigned. There was equal disquiet in Kent as Royce and his team waited for news of the test. The fact that the Eagle performed exactly as intended was satisfying to all concerned, but it nevertheless showed that the engine could be further developed, which meant that considerably more work was involved. When the engine burst into life and its speed regulated so as to gradually rise to its maximum, the noise, it is said, could be heard from afar. Derby eventually came to recognise the sound of aero-engines on test at full power, allegedly giving rise to the expression the 'Derby Hum'.

That test exceeded all expectations, and recording the events at Derby, Harold Nockolds in his book *The Magic Of A Name*, indicated that the Eagle, designed for 200hp, actually developed 225bhp. Royce, having examined the data that was sent to him, was careful to question every detail of the test, and wanted assurances on a number of issues. As it happened, Hives was able to follow Royce's instructions with impeccable accuracy, and between them they were quickly able to increase the Eagle's speed to 1,800rpm,

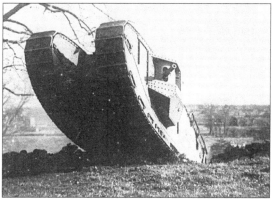

then 2,000rpm, which provided 300bhp, one-third more power than had originally been envisaged. Mervyn O'Gorman had been sceptical of Royce's engine philosophy, but now conceded that Royce had been correct.

The tests led to the Admiralty ordering an initial 25 Eagle engines, deliveries of which began late in 1915. Progressive development had resulted in these engines producing 255bhp at 1,800rpm, although they were able to sustain 1,900rpm for short periods without fear of damage or excessive wear. The first aeroplane to be fitted with the Eagle was the Handley Page 0/100 bomber, and the inaugural flight was made at lunchtime on 18 December 1915 from Hendon aerodrome.

In addition to being fitted to aircraft, the Eagle was also destined to power tanks. The engine's output and flexibility made it suitable for such purposes, and here are illustrated two types of machine, one dating from 1919, and the other, a heavy tank fitted with the Eagle VIII engine. (Courtesy Bovington Tank Museum)

From the Eagle I, as the first engines were known, the basic design evolved into a comprehensive series of aero-engines. Output increased with successive designs, so that by the time the Eagle VIII (recognised as being the most famous of all Eagles) was introduced it was producing 350bhp. In post-war years the Eagle IX was designed for mainly civilian operations; the Eagle XV had a two-speed propeller reduction gear, and the little known XVI bore no relation to previous Eagles, being designed by Rowledge and test bed run in 1926. Each of the Eagle series of engines shared a similarity, having 12-cylinder water-cooled units of 20.32 litres capacity and a 60 degree V formation. Each cylinder with its water jacket formed a separate unit, and each featured a single inlet and exhaust valve along with two sparking plugs.

Henry Royce was proven to be rightly concerned about the design of air-cooled aero-engines, and by the middle of World War One these were showing serious limitations in development. Water-cooled engines were therefore forming the backbone of the Allied fleets, and the majority of these were built by Rolls-Royce. In fairness, Rolls-Royce Eagle engines were not without their problems, and were prone to cooling system leaks. Evidence exists of Handley Page bomber crews having to chew ample amounts of gum in preparation for plugging water leaks in flight!

Hawks, Falcons and Condors

A straight-six Hawk aero-engine that was originally intended to power training

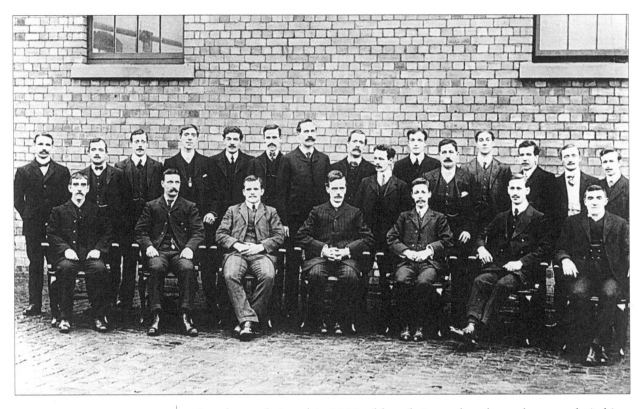

The management team at Nightingale Road pictured in 1919 or 1920. Front row, left to right: *T. Hyde, Matthews, Platford, De Looze, Wormald, T. Nadin, Dagnell.* Back row, left to right: *E. Lupton, Logan, Reeves, -?-, -?-, -?-, Rogers, -?-, W. Ellis, Capt. Hallam, -?-, -?-, -?-, W. Gradwell, J. Roscoe. (Courtesy Sir Henry Royce Memorial Foundation)*

aircraft was designed in 1915, although it was largely used on naval airships. Output rose from a modest 75bhp at 1,350rpm to 91bhp and then to 94bhp before being increased to 105bhp in 1918. Unlike the Eagle, the Hawk was built without a reduction gearbox, the propeller turning at crankshaft speed. The Hawk did not go into production at Derby, but was built under licence at Bristol by Brazil Straker under the direction of Roy Fedden.

The Nightingale Road factory became heavily involved in a third type of aero-engine, the 190hp Falcon V12, which saw service in the renowned Bristol Fighter. Much of the Falcon's design was undertaken by R.W. Harvey-Bailey at Derby, and was, in essence, a scaled-down Eagle engine commensurate with a pair of Hawk engines doubled up. The Falcon was also made by Brazil Straker at Fishponds in Bristol; development was staged so that in April 1916 output was 205bhp at 2,000rpm, increasing to 228bhp the following month, 247bhp in April 1917, rising to 278bhp and finally to 285bhp in July 1918. As the Falcon III the engine remained in service until the 1930s.

The Condor was the last of the Rolls-Royce aero-engines developed during wartime. It was introduced in the late summer of 1918, too late for war action. At 35 litres it was the largest of the Rolls-Royce aero-engines at the time, it had four valves per cylinder instead of two, and although originally intended for heavy bomber aircraft, notably the Handley Page V/1500, it was extensively utilised for both military and civilian operations in peacetime. Series I Condors were specified to produce 550/600bhp, later the IA and III delivered 650bhp. It was the Condor III that became the best known and was fitted to several famous types of aircraft.

Throughout World War One Nightingale Road was working at full capacity designing, building and repairing aero-engines. When Claude Johnson asked the government for help in increasing production capacity this was not immediately forthcoming. Derby was faced with the problem of manufacturing all components, and Johnson argued that by sub-contracting to reliable firms it would be possible to increase engine production. Eventually this did happen, and the National Shell Factory at Derby, along with the National Projectile Factory at Dudley in the West Midlands, was recruited to take on some of Rolls-Royce's work. When Claude Johnson had the opportunity to acquire a factory with the facilities to produce Eagle engines, there was no response from the government. Nor was there any positive reaction when Johnson proposed building a new repair workshop, and it was only when the situation had become so grave that deliveries of aero-engines were falling seriously behind that action was taken. The government requisitioned the Clement-Talbot motor works in London to produce Falcon engines and to repair other Rolls-Royce engines under the direction of Johnson. Ultimately Falcons were never made at the works, and it was aero-engine repairs that were undertaken.

To give some idea of the effort that Rolls-Royce put into wartime activities, some 60 per cent of all British aero-engines were manufactured by the company. The strain on Royce, already an ill man, was considerable. For their wartime work Royce and Arthur Wormald were awarded OBEs; Ernest Hives and R.W. Harvey-Bailey received MBEs. As for Royce, life at St Margaret's Bay had become untenable because of aerial and infantry activity, and when hostilities were at their height Royce and Ethel Aubin moved to the more peaceful location of Elmstead, West Wittering. After the war was over Royce and Nurse Aubin escaped to the tranquillity of Le Canadel.

During World War One Rolls-Royce built 3,111 Eagle engines, 206 Hawks and 1,132 Falcons. One hundred Condors were ordered for the war effort but none were delivered during the hostilities.

CHAPTER FIVE

DERBY BETWEEN THE WARS

S OME TIME before the Armistice, Claude Johnson became apprehensive about the future activities of Rolls-Royce. Both he and Rolls-Royce chairman Ernest Claremont were concerned that following hostilities the company might find itself producing aero-engines for just one customer, the government. While aero-engine manufacturing during the war was potentially lucrative, that situation could not be expected to continue. As it happened, Johnson and Claremont were right to be concerned, and events proved that some firms in a similar situation felt the chill wind of the withdrawal of government financing, and ultimately faced bankruptcy.

Rolls-Royce became synonymous with aero-engines during and after World War One. Here Eric Platford is seen examining one of the Eagle engines fitted to Alcock and Brown's Vickers Vimy aeroplane, which completed the first non-stop crossing of the Atlantic in June 1919. Platford had been sent to Newfoundland to prepare the engines prior to the pilots' heroic flight. (Courtesy Sir Henry Royce Memorial Foundation)

No one at Rolls-Royce expected there to be a resurgence of the luxury car market after the war. Claude Johnson was convinced that the future lay in forging a partnership with a suitable American company to design and manufacture aero-engines. It was J.B. Duke, the tobacco magnate and Rolls-Royce shareholder, who Johnson thought the most appropriate ally, and he went to the United States with much anticipation.

Claude Johnson's expedition to America lasted nine months, during which time he experienced several failures. Negotiations with J.B. Duke faltered, and Johnson was reluctant to allow any other manufacturer to build Rolls-Royce engines for fear of them becoming a rival company. Thoughts in the US were, however, mainly directed towards production of the Liberty engine, and assistance was offered in this respect

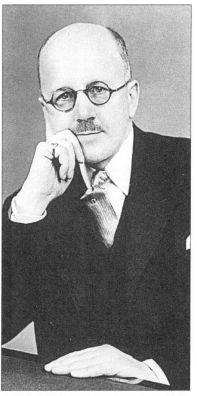

Joining Rolls-Royce from Napier in 1920, Arthur Sidgreaves (later Sir Arthur) was appointed as export manager and in 1929 succeeded Basil Johnson (brother of Claude Johnson) as managing director. Sidgreaves took many decisions that assured Rolls-Royce of the high profile it still enjoys today. (Courtesy Sir Henry Royce Memorial Foundation)

Royce with Albert Elliott and Charles Jenner, discussing the performance of this 20hp prototype car in 1920. Elliott worked closely with Royce and in 1937, after Royce's death in 1933, was appointed chief engineer. (Courtesy Sir Henry Royce Memorial Foundation)

courtesy of Maurice Olley and Ernest Hives, with Johnson's complete agreement. The design of the Liberty did not materialise as had been planned, and the American engineers working on the project preferred not to listen to the advice suggested by Rolls-Royce. The result was that the Liberty failed miserably to perform, and ultimately all the development work was for nothing.

The one American car-maker that was considered to be in the same league as Rolls-Royce was Pierce-Arrow, which was also a manufacturer of commercial vehicles. Johnson thought that if Rolls-Royce were to seriously break into the American market, then it was with Pierce-

Above: Royce, pictured in 1921 with a 40/50hp. During the inter-war years Royce only visited Derby on one occasion; his time was spent working from his home on the south coast of England in the summer months, and in winter at Le Canadel. (Courtesy Sir Henry Royce Memorial Foundation)

Right: The dynamometer test house at Nightingale Road in 1923. At this time the 40/50hp remained in production and was joined by the newly introduced 20hp. Compare this picture with those showing the dynamometer test house in a previous chapter. (Courtesy Sir Henry Royce Memorial Foundation)

Bottom: This is the 20hp test house, as photographed in 1923. Rolls-Royce manufactured all the necessary components for its chassis apart from batteries, magnetos and sparking plugs. It was generally accepted that components made at Derby were of higher quality than those used on most other cars at the time. Following initial assembly an engine was run-in on coal gas for as long as six hours, after which it was subjected to dynamometer testing. Road testing was then undertaken for some 50 miles, and when the car was returned to the test shop the engine would be decarbonised. When this photograph was taken Rolls-Royce employed some 3,500 people. (Courtesy Sir Henry Royce Memorial Foundation)

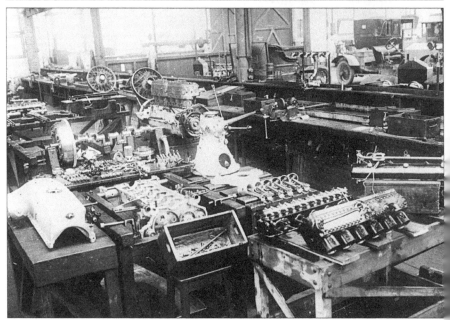

Arrow that an alliance should be forged. Pursuing talks with the company, it was Johnson's opinion that each party could benefit from the other and share expertise: Rolls-Royce would use the Pierce-Arrow organisation to sell Rolls-Royce motor cars in the US, thus avoiding direct competition, and in return Rolls-Royce would market Pierce-Arrow trucks in Britain and Europe. Again, nothing came of Johnson's ventures.

Derby, in a similar way to all other towns and cities throughout Britain, celebrated the Armistice in joyous fashion. At Nightingale Road there were celebrations too, but the underlying task was to quickly return to business as usual. Claude Johnson's pessimism regarding the future of aero-engine technology proved to be more or less correct, and despite aviation having changed the way of the world to some great extent, the British government foresaw that such advances in wartime had little to do with civilian aviation in peacetime.

Aviation technology did not entirely recede after the war, and the spirits of millions of people on both sides of the Atlantic were boosted when Captain John Alcock and Lieutenant Arthur Whitten Brown pioneered the first non-stop crossing of the ocean between the 14 and 15 June 1919. Leaving Newfoundland, their overloaded Rolls-Royce Eagle-engined Vickers Vimy Bomber was quickly engulfed in fog and cloud, and despite stalling the aeroplane because of being totally disorientated, not to mention being at the

Nightingale Road in the early 1920s with the 20hp under construction. A feature of the 20hp was its centre gear selector, something that many customers, who were more used to a right-hand gear lever, disapproved of. When this photograph was taken Rolls-Royce employees, according to their experience, could expect to earn between £3 and £4 per week. It was customary to take on premium apprentices, whose parents would pay the company £400 for a four-year apprenticeship. The regime at Nightingale Road was strict, something that made for good discipline. (Courtesy Sir Henry Royce Memorial Foundation)

*Henry Royce at the wheel of
46PK, the first New Phantom
(Phantom 1). The location is
Elmstead, Royce's home at West
Wittering. Royce used the car
extensively. Dated 1925, the
photograph is signed by Royce.
(Courtesy Rolls-Royce & Bentley
Motor Cars Ltd)*

mercy of a faulty airspeed indicator, Alcock, just 100 feet from the waves, wrestled with the controls and regained power. After 16 hours and 28 minutes flying time, during which they flew 1,890 miles, the pilots landed nose-down in an Irish bog in County Galway. Needless to say the Rolls-Royce Eagle engines had performed without any hesitation. It was largely Alcock and Brown's feat that highlighted the role civil aviation offered.

It was not only Alcock and Brown, both of whom were knighted (Alcock was killed six months after the epic flight when he crash landed in thick fog near Rouen in France), that received adulation. Vickers, too, won much acclaim, and once more Rolls-Royce was in the spotlight. Nobody was more elated than the workforce at Nightingale Road who had built the Eagle engines, and as a means of celebration the factory was closed for a day, and the whole of Derby was in festive mood.

More Silver Ghosts

During wartime, motor cars, and the Silver Ghost in particular, had not been completely forgotten at Nightingale Road in the rush to develop and build aero-engines. The 40/50hp chassis had remained in production, albeit for military applications only, until 1917. There is evidence that soon after production of the 40/50hp had ceased, Royce and his closest design team began to think about resuming car making once hostilities had ended. Rolls-Royce's 'one-model' policy dictated that once car production could be implemented, it would be the Silver Ghost that would continue to carry the company's insignia. If Royce and his engineers had even the slightest apprehension about making available a design that was then already 12 years old, they need not have worried. Elsewhere in the motor industry there had been little or no development during the war years, and virtually every other car maker faced a similar dilemma.

World War One had confirmed that motor vehicles had a positive role to play in the 20th century, and a serious demand for them emerged as hostilities ended. There was, therefore, a proliferation of companies eager to satisfy the desire for the newfound independence that motor cars provided, many of

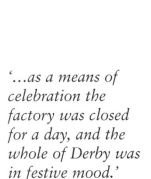

*'...as a means of
celebration the
factory was closed
for a day, and the
whole of Derby was
in festive mood.'*

After Claude Johnson's death the senior management established a memorial to the man who has since become known as the hyphen in Rolls-Royce. Pictured in around 1929 at Derby can be seen (from left to right) *Eric Platford, R.W. Harvey-Bailey, Harry Swift, Arthur Wormald, Arthur Sidgreaves, William Cowen, Ernest Hives, Capt. Hallam, John De Looze and Tom Haldenby.* (Courtesy Sir Henry Royce Memorial Foundation)

which diversified from war effort manufacturing. Some highly respected names appeared during the war's aftermath, one being Alvis, and Bentley another. The latter, of course, became synonymous with Rolls-Royce, particularly after World War Two, remaining thus until the family of motor cars was separated in what transpired to be an acrimonious business deal concerning Rolls-Royce, the Vickers Company, Volkswagen, and BMW.

The war over, confidence returned and something of a boom was experienced. The feel-good situation was not to last, and before the end of 1920 economic depression had set in. During the intervening period, however, Claude Johnson's pessimism about the market for luxury cars was proved unfounded, and pre-war Silver Ghosts, including those not in particularly pristine condition, fetched prices well above their original values. One reason for the Silver Ghost's popularity was its quality and reliability, proven beyond all doubt by its efficient service in the desert.

As if Johnson and Royce had foreseen the vagaries of the economic climate, and that in their opinion the demand for expensive luxury cars would be largely diminished post-war, they instigated the development of a new but smaller Rolls-Royce in secret at Elmstead. In Rolls-Royce fashion the development of any new model is a protracted affair, for every detail has to be exhaustively tested to destruction before the definitive product emerges from the drawing board. In the meantime, production of the Silver Ghost was resumed, and as well as the Alpine trials modifications, some of those arising from military operations were also effected.

Although the Nightingale Road factory had been kept busy during the war with regard to armoured vehicles, there was nevertheless much work involved in preparing the works for a resumption of chassis production. Rolls-Royce had

Above: Chassis 10EX at Brooklands in 1927, when Roy Robotham was conducting speed trials. A prototype for the New Phantom, the car lapped Brooklands at a speed in excess of 91mph. (Courtesy Sir Henry Royce Memorial Foundation)

Right: The 20/25hp was introduced in 1929 as successor to the 20hp. Pictured during that year at Derby are Eric Platford and Arthur Wormald, testing one of the new 20/25hp chassis. Fitted to the chassis is a slave body that was used for testing purposes, and as such the vehicle was known as a test rig. The date over the door of the workshop is 1910. (Courtesy Sir Henry Royce Memorial Foundation)

a nicely balanced order book – there were back orders for the 40/50hp, and the number of new orders indicated that production should be increased to a level above that of the 500 chassis per year relating to pre-1914 days – but information from government sources promised a glitch on the horizon. Winston Churchill, then Chancellor of the Exchequer, imposed a swingeing tax on car users that made motoring very much more expensive than it had previously been. Motorists were having to pay a Road Tax equal to £1 per engine horsepower.

A further issue that concerned the Rolls-Royce board was that some pressure was being exerted on the company to form a merger with another car manufacturer, and indeed the idea of a consortium of several manufacturers had been tabled. It was presumed that the pressure emanated from the government, the view being taken that by amalgamating different aspects of the motor industry, foreign competition, especially from America, would be largely vanquished. When Claude Johnson attended a meeting chaired by a highly respected firm of accountants, he found himself in the company of directors of Daimler, Wolseley, and Vickers. At least one other manufacturer, Sunbeam, had declined an invitation to attend.

Vickers was already highly respected as an aircraft manufacturer, having been invited in 1908 to construct airships for the Admiralty. The firm began building aircraft in 1911 at Erith in Kent, and it was Vickers that had provided some of the weaponry and armour for those Silver Ghosts pressed into service during the war. Claude Johnson was most unhappy at the prospect of a merger, fearing that it was Vickers' intention to acquire Rolls-Royce through the back door. Johnson's perception was further boosted by the fact that three of Vickers' directors were present at the meeting, and that the spokesman, Sir Victor Caillard, was intent on obtaining some of Rolls-Royce's manufacturing statistics. Incensed by the nature of the meeting, Johnson stridently voiced his

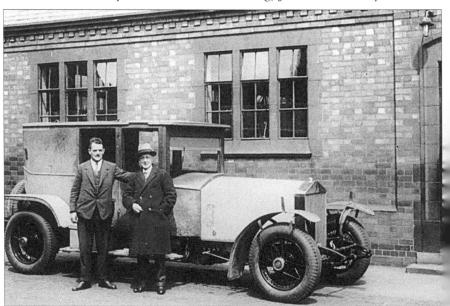

view that he would rather see Rolls-Royce go out of business than succumb to Vickers' advances. The events of later years are therefore of interest!

Rolls-Royce Remain in the Aero-Engine Business

During the months immediately following the Armistice, Royce had declared that Rolls-Royce should remain in the aero-engine business, both in terms of civil and military applications. Royce was not the only person to anticipate that domestic air services would emerge from the war years, and in February 1919 the world's first continuous scheduled service was inaugurated in Germany when Deutsche Luft Reederei linked Berlin with Leipzig and Weimar. A month later a service was established in Belgium, and in August the same year regular flights between London and Paris began when Air Transport & Travel Ltd launched their daily schedule using a de Havilland DH4. This was only the start, and with more and more services becoming available, there was a demand for aircraft, which naturally called for aero-engines.

Photographed together in 1929 are R.J. Mitchell and Henry Royce. Between them they strove to acquire the Schneider Trophy for Britain for all time. Mitchell was the designer of the Supermarine S6 and subsequently the Spitfire. Royce designed the R engine, which powered the Supermarine floatplane, along with the design that emerged as the PV12 and Merlin. Mitchell died before the Spitfire went into service, and Royce did not live to see the Merlin go into action. (Courtesy Sir Henry Royce Memorial Foundation)

1919 and 1920 were the years of adventure and exploration: following Alcock and Brown's epic North Atlantic flight, brothers Ross and Keith Smith made the first flight from Britain to Australia, 11,130 miles in 124 hours flying time, again in an Eagle-engined Vimy aeroplane. Another Eagle Vimy propelled Van Ryneveld and Quintin Brand from England to South Africa in 1920, the 6,328 miles being covered in a little under 93 hours.

The Eagle family of engines included the Condor, which was famous for powering Sir Alan Cobham's Short Singapore flying boat, which so successfully flew overland from England to South Africa, and return, covering some 22,000 miles without incident. The 35-litre 600hp Condor eventually gave way to an altogether new type of engine, the 2-litre 490hp Kestrel, development work having commenced in 1925. With the introduction of the Kestrel there was formed the basis of a whole series of aero-engines that were manufactured throughout the inter-war years.

Aero-engine design played an important role in the post-war Silver Ghost, inasmuch as aluminium pistons were adopted, the technology of which was similar to those used in the Eagle. Applying aluminium pistons to the 40/50hp engine posed a number of difficulties for the Derby engineers, and solving them involved some intensive work on behalf of A.G. Elliott at West Wittering, and Hives and his experimental crew at Nightingale Road. The engine was demonstrating piston slap, and in Elliott's opinion the remedy called for a piston having a hydraulically loaded pad in its skirt. Furthermore, the oil feed to the gudgeon pin could be used to provide the hydraulic energy. Hives did not entirely share Elliott's philosophy, and sought an alternative solution; trial and error prevailed and the resulting technology, known as the split skirt, was patented in Hives' name.

A New Chassis Range

Royce and his design team took a pragmatic approach towards motor cars after 1918, and not only did they concentrate on developing the 20hp, but they also

The fact that Henry Royce spent much of his time in southern France meant that the situation was ideal for intensive testing of experimental cars. Derby personnel would often make the journey to Le Canadel, either to prove engineering, or to deliver a car to Royce for his evaluation. Here Royce is seen with his constant companion Nurse Ethel Aubin and two of his closest associates, Ernest Hives and, on the far right, Albert Elliott. (Courtesy Rolls-Royce & Bentley Motor Cars Ltd)

resumed research into larger horsepower cars, of similar size and concept to the 40/50hp Silver Ghost, which were given the 'EX' notation. The EX chassis range materialised into such cars as the Phantoms, with development continuing until well into the post-World War Two years, by which time the chassis division had moved away from Derby to be established at Crewe. The smaller range of chassis was allocated a 'G' notation, which stood for 'Goshawk', thus maintaining the wartime policy of naming aero-engines after birds of prey.

In his biography of Henry Royce, Donald Bastow relates how the West Wittering design team devised provisional sketches of the proposed car in four days, and how detailed specifications were completed within three weeks. There is evidence that much of the initial work was finalised by the middle of March 1919, in readiness for detailed work to begin at Nightingale Road.

There are some interesting aspects of the design of the 20hp, inasmuch as the engine was influenced by aero-engine technology. Additionally it is evident that savings in manufacturing costs in comparison to the larger and more powerful cars were not as expected because overheads remained similar whatever the parameters. Early designs had called for a six-cylinder engine of around three litres capacity with overhead valves and two overhead camshafts, but this was found not to operate as efficiently as had been proposed. Following modifications it was an engine of 3,127cc with pushrod-operated valves that emerged. Only one experimental chassis was completed at Derby to the earlier design, and from what little evidence exists, it can be presumed that the vehicle, which was completed sometime during 1920, was never registered. The second chassis was complete by the autumn of 1921, and the interesting feature of the car was its three-speed gearbox and central gear selector, both of which were unseen on the 40/50hp. It was customary for Rolls-Royce cars to feature right-hand gear selection, but the adoption of a centrally positioned gear lever was deemed to be more practical, and avoided costly modifications when building left-hand drive vehicles.

There is no hiding the fact that Royce considered the three-speed gearbox preferable to a four-speed affair, as long as the engine's torque curve was sufficiently matched to the gear ratios. It appears that Royce's philosophy was not always greeted with equal enthusiasm from every quarter, nevertheless, in America, for instance, three-speed boxes were universally favoured. Criticism of three-speed gearboxes was voiced not only by some Derby personnel, but also by a number of commentators who thought the car emulated the Buick. Building the 20hp engine at Nightingale Road called for some forward-thinking technology, in that the design comprised a monobloc cylinder arrangement along with a detachable cylinder head cast as a single piece. The engine's cooling system was advanced for its time, the water passages being carefully designed so as to provide the greatest efficiency.

The 20/25hp engine saw a number of applications including light tanks. Originally fitted with a Meadows engine, this Mk II tank performed exceptionally well when fitted with a Rolls-Royce engine. (Courtesy Bovington Tank Museum)

Following its introduction it became evident that the 20hp suffered from a number of relatively minor problems. Some, such as the carburetion and an unacceptable level of vibration, were sufficiently acute as to require the attention of the design team at West Wittering, but the majority were dealt with at Nightingale Road by the experimental department. Development continued through trial and error, and Ernest Hives arranged for adjustments to be made during production.

In time the traditionalists had their way and in 1925 the 20hp underwent a number of more serious technical modifications. Right-hand drive cars were fitted with a right-hand gear change – left-hand drive cars retained the central lever – and the gearbox featured four speeds instead of three. The adoption of four-speed gearboxes substantially raised the car's weight, which compromised the 20hp's performance, a feature that was already the object of some harsh criticism. Front wheel brakes were also specified from 1925, a year or so after this feature had appeared on the 40/50hp. Previously all models had relied on rear-wheel brakes, the hand brake operating duplicate shoes on the same axle.

Despite the 20hp attracting a reputation for having a tardy performance, it sold well, and was especially popular with what were referred to as the 'professional classes'. There was every reason for the car to be a popular choice, for it became possible to acquire a new Rolls-Royce for around half the price a Silver Ghost would command. In an analogous situation, when Rolls-Royce introduced the Bentley Eight in 1984 it was immediately more widely available to those customers who had previously considered Rolls-Royce and Bentley ownership to be out of reach. Similarly, following the divergence of Rolls-Royce and Bentley, Volkswagen made it known that it intended to introduce a new and smaller model, codenamed the MSB (mid-size Bentley), in order to make Bentley ownership available to a wider clientele.

The sales teams in London and at Derby were well-versed in supplying cars to the most discerning of customers, such as Lord Baden-Powell, seen here alongside his 20/25hp. (Courtesy Sir Henry Royce Memorial Foundation)

Within the company, the 20hp was not universally appreciated. While Ernest Hives and his experimental department engineers sought to develop the 20hp along with future models, the London sales team remained somewhat unenthusiastic about it. Unofficially Conduit Street displayed a measure of scepticism, preferring to persuade customers to select the 40/50hp wherever possible. So bigoted were some of the sales personnel that rather than sell a new 20hp, they would go out of their way to market previously used cars. Some of the Derby personnel referred to the car's perceived

unhurried performance in none too fond terms, but this did not detract from the fact that the 20hp was an extraordinarily fine car. Enjoying an impressive survival rate, those 20hps still in use give their owners unequalled service and comfort. The fact that 2,940 20hps were sold is sufficient proof that Royce and his teams at West Wittering and Derby had the right formula, although it was not apparent to everybody at the time.

Arguments about the 20hp's performance reigned for some time, and there is evidence that Hives at Derby did not always share Royce's beliefs. While the two had the highest regard for each other, Hives nevertheless questioned Royce's decision to adopt a 3-litre engine, which was smaller than most of the car's contemporaries and therefore put it at a disadvantage when it came to out and out competition. Showing his annoyance, Royce retorted appropriately, defending his conviction that the car's weight should be kept to no more than 35cwt, which in fact was seldom the case. Royce was adamant that spare wheel mounts should not be fitted on the front wings and running boards, as was then popular, but at the rear to ensure the weight was removed from the front axle. Further evidence of Royce's displeasure can be detected from a memo sent to Arthur Wormald and Ernest Hives at Derby. Fearing that the sales department were ignoring his advice, Royce effectively issued an ultimatum: 'While I am able I shall take enormous interest in our production, but naturally I shall not continue to do so if I find the information collected, and recommendations, ruthlessly wasted.' Royce was also emphatic in that he considered it 'inconceivable that the Company should have a Chief Engineer, and then not take such engineer's advice...'

From Ghosts to Phantoms

In May 1925 Rolls-Royce announced the successor to the 40/50hp Silver Ghost, the New Phantom, which became universally known as the Phantom I. Much of the bodywork design for the Phantom I is credited to a young man who had joined Rolls-Royce in 1916, met Henry Royce in 1917, and was transferred to the airship design office for the duration of the war, where he gained immeasurable experience. Returning to Rolls-Royce after the war, Ivan Evernden was chosen by Royce to work alongside him at Elmstead in the design studio, and it was from there that his relationship with Nightingale Road was nurtured. Evernden's work brought him into contact with all the respected coachbuilders, and his mark is not only associated with the Phantoms but all subsequent Rolls-Royce (and Bentley after 1931) models until 1952, when the Bentley R-Type Continental made its debut.

The Phantom I was, in a number of respects, an updated 40/50hp. Technically, the most noteworthy features were the engine, which had some 20hp influence, and the torque tube type transmission, which had a plate clutch instead of the Silver Ghost's cone arrangement. The gear box fitted to the Phantom I featured spirally-cut gears for the final drive bevels, a refinement found on the very last of the Silver Ghosts. The Phantom's 7,668cc engine was of slightly smaller bore than that of the Silver Ghost, and the stroke was longer; significantly, it was an enlarged version of the engine fitted to the smaller Rolls-Royce 20hp, although the cylinder arrangement was similar to that of the 40/50hp.

Phantom Is were fitted with vertical radiator shutters, hand controlled from the driving position, and some Silver Ghost owners changing to the new model deplored the fact that the thermostatic cooling system fitted to late model 40/50s was discontinued. The Phantom I did have a number of refinements over the Silver Ghost, but these were largely overshadowed by the criticisms the car attracted, which, arguably, were often unfounded. Nevertheless, the Phantom I was relatively short-lived, and for years the model was somewhat ignored by Rolls-Royce enthusiasts who preferred either the Silver Ghost or the Phantom II.

When design work on the Phantom II began late in 1927, Rolls-Royce had already suffered the loss of the company's greatest architect, Claude Johnson, who died on 11 April 1926 at the age of 63. Claude Johnson's death, caused to a great extent by overwork and stress, was not only a severe blow to those at Conduit Street and Nightingale Road, but Henry Royce had also lost a friend and stalwart colleague. There is every reason to suppose that had it not been for Claude Johnson's appetite for work, together with his organising talents, Rolls-Royce might well not have survived after Rolls's death and Royce's long and incapacitating illness. Claude Johnson can also be thanked for the now famous Grecian Temple radiator shell. As early as 1922 Royce had wanted to do away with the feature, favouring a more rational design, and one that was less expensive to produce. Johnson would not hear of it and persuaded Royce that such a feature was not only distinctive, but also conveyed more than a measure of individualism.

European testing meant that Derby personnel were often away from Nightingale Road for relatively long periods. There were, nevertheless, occasions when test drivers, who were usually skilled mechanics, required the assistance of the factory's experimental department. In such cases experimental engineers would be despatched to repair cars at the company's premises at Chateauroux, or to a Rolls-Royce agent. Although pictured in France, the location of the photograph is unclear; note the size of the Rolls-Royce compared to the Citroën C4/6 behind it, itself not a small car. (Courtesy Rolls-Royce & Bentley Motor Cars Ltd)

Before his death, Claude Johnson had invited his younger brother Basil to join Rolls-Royce and to take on some of his work. Basil took over as managing director after Claude's demise, but he did not retain that position for any length of time. Lacking much of his brother's resourcefulness, there is some evidence of mistrust between himself and Royce, and in 1929 he was persuaded to take early retirement. Succeeding Basil Johnson, Arthur Sidgreaves was appointed to the post of managing director, having previously been appointed as export manager on joining Rolls-Royce in 1920 from Napier.

The 20/25hp

In 1929 the 20hp, deemed to be obsolete, was succeeded by the 20/25hp. The model supported a number of features that were fresh, not least the engine with its bore increased to 3 inches and compression raised from 4.6:1 to 5.25:1. The crankshaft, too, was new, allowing the engine to run at greater rpm. Modifications were made to the chassis, and along with a revised gearbox casing features included a taller radiator supporting vertical shutters. The latter was welcomed by customers and motoring journalists alike, as the feature arguably improved the car's appearance. The brakes were modified to give improved performance, and the larger section tyres enhanced road-holding. In terms of success, the 20/25 was the most popular of the Rolls-Royce models of the inter-war period, with 3,824 cars sold.

Throughout its span of production, the 20/25 underwent continual modification in accordance with advancing technology together with the constant experimental work conducted at Nightingale Road. Of huge interest to customers, and latterly to marque enthusiasts, is the variety of coachwork fitted to the 20/25 chassis. All the leading coachbuilders at the time were naturally associated with the model, and a considerable number of other firms who were not always directly connected to Rolls-Royce were also commissioned to supply bodies. In total, 110 coachbuilders offered coachwork for the 20/25 chassis, and a number of others were responsible for re-bodying. The styles of coachwork to be seen on the 20/25 therefore range from the formal sedancalette (that by Hooper on chassis GGP3 is a fine example) to the rakish lines of GLG73, a Salmons 3-position drop head coupé.

The 20/25hp engine was used in a series of light tanks, which were approved for Army use in 1929. Modifications were necessary before the engines could be installed in the tanks, which were constructed by a number of manufacturers including Vickers, Vickers-Armstrong, and Royal Ordnance. The experimental department was involved in the preparation work, which included devising new oil pumps and filters, a modified sump, revised carburetion and the fitting of a starter on the off-side of the engine rather than the near-side. Meadows six-cylinder engines were originally specified for use in the tanks, but when the Rolls-Royce engine was installed it was necessary to fit it in reverse so that the front of the engine faced rearwards. The 20/25 engine was mated to a Wilson pre-selector gearbox, and a three-belt pulley attached to the end of the crankshaft allowed for the use of auxiliary equipment. The usual exhaust manifold was modified to that of a straight outlet.

The Rolls-Royce powered tanks accommodated a crew of two and were

Photographed in France with an experimental Phantom II are Roy Robotham (left), Eric Platford and John Maddox. Continental testing was considered an essential aspect of ensuring that Rolls-Royce motor cars offered customers the most reliable and efficient service. The tradition of testing cars throughout mainland Europe stemmed from an incident when a Silver Ghost failed to start on a steep hill while being driven in mountainous country. Previous testing over some of Britain's most demanding roads proved insufficient in respect of the conditions that could be expected to be encountered over passes in such places as the Alps. (Courtesy Sir Henry Royce Memorial Foundation)

fitted with a Vickers .303 machine gun. Appointed mainly for service in the Middle East, a number were sent to Palestine in 1936. According to surviving records, at least one of the tanks remained there until 1940, when it was pressed into action in France. The top speed of the tank was around 30mph. There is evidence that during the experimental department's research on the tank programme, road testing was conducted not only around the Nightingale Road works, but also throughout the surrounding area on some of Derbyshire's country lanes.

The work on light tanks served as something of a precursor to later developments when Rolls-Royce was heavily involved in the design of heavy tanks for use during World War Two. As for the light tanks, Tom C. Clarke refers to the 20/25 engine not performing as might have been hoped, the cause for this being unclear, but possibly attributed to either overloading of the vehicles or inadequate filtration under desert conditions.

In September 1929 the Phantom II was announced after a gestation period of only two years, an outstanding feat considering the time it would normally have taken Rolls-Royce to prepare a new model. First and foremost, the Phantom II was intended to compete directly with rival models. The Phantom I had, by this time, come to be regarded as outmoded, especially its chassis, which displayed front-axle tramping characteristics. Considered by many enthusiasts to be the finest of the Derby Rolls-Royces, the Phantom II featured an all-new chassis with a 7,668cc six-cylinder engine. The two blocks of three cast-iron cylinders were on an aluminium crankcase, together with a one-piece aluminium head. The valves were of the overhead type and push-rod operated. Much about the chassis design was similar to the 20hp and the 20/25, but a feature seen on the Phantom II was its centralised lubrication system, something which remained on Rolls-Royce and Bentley models well into the post-war years.

The fact that development of the Phantom II was conducted within such an impressively short timescale is a credit to the experimental department at Nightingale Road, and the intense road testing that was conducted both at home and in France. Road-testing headquarters had been established in the town of Chateauroux, which is midway between the Loire valley and Limoges. As a route centre the town is ideal, since it is at the hub of nine roads, thus making it possible to alternate testing over a variety of road surfaces and conditions.

The first experimental Phantom II,18EX, was on the road in early December 1928, and the second prototype chassis, 19EX, was in service with Royce at Le Canadel only one month later. That same month 20EX was in the care of the experimental department, and in February 1929 21EX served as a general training and experimental vehicle that was ultimately used in London at the Rolls-Royce School of Instruction. Throughout production experiment and development remained prime issues, giving rise to a number of modifications effected until 1936 and the introduction of Rolls-Royce's most refined, if not complicated, Derby-built motor car, the Phantom III.

Possibly the most desirable Phantom is the Phantom II Continental, the name given to those 281 short-chassis cars that were designed by Ivan Evernden. Royce accepted that the long straight roads of France were suitable for a measure of fast touring that was simply not possible on the winding, narrow roads of Britain. Whereas a Phantom might often be chauffeur driven, a Phantom II Continental would almost certainly be the domain of the owner-driver, and it offered the highest levels of comfort for both the driver and passengers. Employing a shorter chassis kept the car's weight to a minimum, and therefore enhanced performance. Ride comfort was achieved by accommodating passengers well within the wheelbase, which meant that in order to compensate for any loss of leg room, foot-wells under the front seats were provided. An altogether more relaxed driving position was created by lowering the height of the steering wheel, realized by reducing the rake of the steering column.

The suspension of the Phantom II Continental benefited from having modified springing. Rolls-Royce was careful to instruct coachbuilders to maintain a low centre of gravity in the bodywork, and to avoid fitting the spare wheel, or wheels, at the rear of the car where tools and luggage were stowed. Phantom IIs were chosen by the most discerning Rolls-Royce customers, and as may be expected the bespoke coachwork on these cars, which was produced by only the most reputable coachbuilders, was often exotic to say the least. Leading personalities at the time who chose the Phantom II included the racing drivers Malcolm Campbell and Woolf Barnato, aircraft pioneers Tommy Sopwith and Glen Kidston; Lord Mountbatten, the Prince of Wales (the future Edward VIII), Princess Mary, Bernard Docker, Charlie Chaplin and Noel Coward.

The Schneider Trophy

A prestigious achievement, for both Rolls-Royce and the British nation, also came in 1929. This was the winning of the Schneider Trophy, which at the time was the foremost accolade in the world of aviation. After the end of World War One the development of aero-engines, as far as Rolls-Royce was concerned, had been largely static, the technology in the market being shared with rival companies Armstrong-Siddeley, Bristol and Napier, the latter having relinquished production of motor cars in 1925.

Following the success of the Eagle, Hawk, Falcon and Condor engines, it was decided that Rolls-Royce should develop an entirely different type of aero-engine, and to help do this one of Napier's most respected engineers was recruited to Nightingale Road. Arthur Rowledge joined Rolls-Royce in 1923 having been responsible for designing the Napier Lion engine, one of the finest aero-engines in aviation history. In their search for a senior designer Rolls-Royce had initially asked Roy Fedden to join the company, but he declined. So did Mark Birkigt, who ultimately chose to stay at Hispano Suiza. As assistant chief engineer to Henry Royce, Rowledge established his office at Nightingale Road, from where he set about modifying the design of the Condor to present the Condor III. Rowledge also became associated with Rolls-Royce motor cars, and was instrumental in designing the servo-assisted braking system for the Phantom II.

In 1925 work began designing the 'F' engine, which was a radical departure from previous Rolls-Royce aero-engines. Having two banks of six cylinders formed from a single aluminium-alloy block, the engine, with its 21.24-litre capacity packed into an extremely compact design, eventually became known as the Kestrel. Completing its official 100-hour test at the first attempt in June 1927, development was concentrated on more advanced versions. The Kestrel powered many of the RAF's fighters during the late 1920s and early 1930s, one of the most famous being Sydney Camm's Hawker Fury.

A larger and more powerful version of the Kestrel was the 36-litre Buzzard, which originally was known as the 'H' engine. One of the features of the Buzzard was its moderate supercharging, which was essential for its intended application powering flying boats, and the demand for high power during take-off. Buzzard engines were used to propel the Short Singapore and Handley Page HP46, among others.

The late 1920s were significant for Rolls-Royce's commitment to Britain's bid to win the Schneider Trophy, an event which, since its inception in December 1912, had been responsible for pushing the limits in aviation technology further than any other. The trophy was presented by the Frenchman Jacques Schneider to encourage development of the seaplane, then considered by him to represent the future in air travel, and the contest to acquire it was initially staged at Monaco in 1913. The event was won by Maurice Prévost, fittingly a fellow Frenchman, in a Gnome rotary engined monoplane with which he achieved a speed of 45.75mph. The following year the trophy, which portrayed a female form diving to kiss a crested wave, was presented to the Briton Howard Pixton in recognition of his achievement flying a Sopwith Tabloid floatplane, again at Monaco, when he averaged almost 87mph, only a little under twice the speed that Prévost had attained.

Jacques Schneider had laid down a number of conditions of entry for the trophy: the competition had to be conducted over water; the participating aircraft were to be seaworthy, and all entrants were required to have the sponsorship of a governing body. The rules also stated that a country was limited to entering three contestants, that the successful nation would host the event the following year, and that winning the trophy outright called for three consecutive victories. That the trophy resides in Britain is thanks to Henry Royce and his loyal team at Nightingale Road, together with R.J. Mitchell. Competitors were required to fly a number of laps around a closed circuit, the entire event totalling some 350 kilometres. There were no competitions during World War One, and it was left to Britain to host the 1919 race, which was held in Bournemouth Bay and dogged by fog and poor weather. Italy won both the 1920 and 1921 events that were staged off Venice, and the following year, Bay of Naples being the venue, it was Britain that was victorious. For the 1922 race the Supermarine Company had entered its new flying boat, Sea Lion II, which was powered by a Napier Lion engine. The designer of the seaplane was R.J. Mitchell, who had joined Supermarine in 1917 aged 22. Preparations for the event were conducted in the utmost secrecy, and no one apart from a mere four people knew that the aeroplane, dismantled and stowed in packing cases, had been quietly shipped to Italy from Southampton.

R.J. Mitchell is synonymous not only with the Schneider Trophy but also with one of the most famous aircraft of all time, the Spitfire. It was 1927 before the trophy was again in British hands, this time courtesy of Mitchell's S5, a development of his S4 monoplane, piloted by Flight Lieutenant S.N. Webster. Thereafter the race was held every two years in order to allow countries sufficient time to develop their machines. For 1929 Mitchell specified the S6, and instead of using the Napier engine, which was considered to have reached the peak of its development, he turned to Napier's rival Rolls-Royce. The decision to move away from Napier was a difficult one, and Mitchell did not choose to do so entirely on his own. He consulted Major Bulman who, on behalf of the Air Ministry, was responsible for the development of aero-engines and knew exactly what Rolls-Royce at Nightingale Road could achieve. Major Bulman considered Rolls-Royce completely capable of building an engine suitable for Mitchell's needs, and believed that it stood a very good chance of powering the S5 to victory. Mitchell had had few dealings with Rolls-Royce until then, and he knew little about the company. Therefore it was with some trepidation that he visited West Wittering and met not only Royce, but also his senior designers, A.J. Rowledge, A.C. Lovesey and Ernest Hives. That meeting was highly significant: Mitchell and Royce were impressed by each other's knowledge and expertise, and Mitchell's close association with Rolls-Royce, which lasted throughout his life, is now well recognised.

The outcome of the meeting between Royce and Mitchell was development of the 'R' engine, itself a development of the Buzzard. Although the R engine shared many of the Buzzard's features, it was quite different in appearance, much emphasis being placed on the reduction of cross-sectional area to aid streamlining. It was proposed to incorporate a large centrifugal supercharger, a specially designed forward-facing air-intake supplying the required volume of ram air. An assurance was given that Rolls-Royce could supply a minimum of

1,500hp, and that with the necessary development could achieve 1,900hp with little or no modification of the engine's frontal area.

Rolls-Royce was given only six months in which to produce the engine, a timescale that was amazingly short. To assist with the project, A.J. Rowledge asked for one of the Royal Aircraft Establishment's most experienced supercharging engineers to be recruited to Nightingale Road. Thus Jimmy Ellor joined the aero-engine team at Derby, where he stayed until 1940 when he was posted to Packard in America to help oversee production of the Rolls-Royce Merlin engine. After the war, Ellor returned to Nightingale Road and resumed duties as chief experimental engineer.

The stringent testing of aero-engines at Nightingale Road was, by nature, noisy. From early morning until well after nightfall the droning 'Derby Hum' could be heard up to five miles away.

Around the R engine, Mitchell designed his S6 seaplane, which shared a number of similarities with the S5, although it was larger and the floats were built to accommodate fuel tanks incorporating baffles intended to prevent fuel surge. Further modifications were made, sufficient to propel Flying Officer H.R. Waghorn to victory, averaging 328.65mph over the seven-lap, 218-mile race on 7 September. The constant testing, modifying, and further testing of the R engine was the cause of just as much stress and fatigue for the Nightingale Road engineers as it was for Royce at West Wittering and Mitchell's team at Supermarine and the flying station at Calshot on the Solent. Four engines were built, each in turn being transported to Southampton, where they were subjected to even more stringent testing aboard the S6s, and then returned to Derby where they were dismantled and carefully examined.

There were times when fitters were called back to the factory at short notice to continue urgent work, and at least on one occasion messages were flashed across cinema screens throughout Derby, appealing for engineers to report to Nightingale Road immediately, which they did willingly and without question.

Delivering the engines between Derby and Calshot necessitated the establishment of a rapid and reliable transport system. This was effectively provided by Rolls-Royce, the transport department having prepared a special 'lorry' capable of conveying an R engine. Engines were usually transported at night, and the experimental department's vehicle became known as the Night Phantom. Rumours exist that whenever the Night Phantom set off on its run, police forces along the route were mobilized to ensure the vehicle's safe and rapid voyage. The 'lorry' in question was 12EX, a Phantom I chassis that had originally carried a Torpedo-style body built by Barker. The conversion was undertaken in September 1929 specifically for the R engine and Schneider Trophy project.

The night before race day there was panic among the maintenance crew in charge of the R engine, which by then had been finally installed in the S6 designated to compete for the trophy. A piece of white metal spotted on the electrode of one of the spark plugs spelled serious trouble, meaning that the entire engine would have to be changed, or at the very least, given a block change. The trophy rules forbade the former, and to undertake the latter was impossible without the service of the factory's skilled engineers. It was only when it was discovered that a team of technicians from Nightingale Road had

'...messages were flashed across cinema screens throughout Derby, appealing for engineers to report to Nightingale Road immediately...'

Watching the Schneider Trophy race in 1929 are Tom Haldenby, William Cowen (sales), Arthur Sidgreaves, John De Looze, Frederick Handley Page, Ernest Hives and Eric Platford. (Courtesy Sir Henry Royce Memorial Foundation)

arrived in Southampton to watch the race that it seemed possible that there might be a glimmer of hope. The fitters had been enjoying a night out in Southampton, and being the worse for alcohol, had gone to their hotels. It was past midnight when some of the technicians were located in the Crown Hotel and roused from their beds; while they were being escorted to Calshot the local constabulary succeeded in rounding up the remaining crew from hotels and boarding houses in the vicinity.

The fact that one of the fitters was left-handed meant that he was able to locate the necessary engine parts, which were out of reach of those who were right-handed. Miraculously, and despite the fitters' earlier merrymaking, the engine was repaired with little time to spare, and when Waghorn strapped himself into the seaplane he remained oblivious to the happenings of the night. There was, however, a measure of trepidation when the seaplane's engine was fired, and considerable relief when it was confirmed that all was well. The triumph of winning the event caught the imagination of a nation already suffering the effects of the severe economic depression, and it was almost a cruel act when the government announced the following month that it would not fund the 1931 race. Philip Snowdon, the Chancellor of the Exchequer, who was averse to such nationalistic rivalry, largely influenced the decision. He could see no reason for the exchequer to underwrite what he considered to be a waste of public money. Needless to say a bitter campaign was waged by the media accusing the government of being defeatist and unpatriotic.

Henry Royce was given a baronetcy in the 1930 birthday honours list. In the same year Sir Henry Segrave gained the world water-speed record on Lake Windermere in his Rolls-Royce R-engined boat *Miss England II*, and the widow of a millionaire ship owner, Lady Lucy Houston, generously made available the sum of £100,000 to fund the 1931 Schneider Trophy. Lady Houston was so enraged by the government's decision not to pay out that she donated the money not only as an act of patriotism but also as a means of embarrassing the prime minister, Ramsay Macdonald. The Government was forced to reverse its earlier decision and permit the event to be held. These three occurrences were a tonic to the nation, although sadly Sir Henry Segrave died on 13 June 1930, while attempting to better his record with *Miss England II*.

Sir Henry Royce was invited to design the engine for the 1931 Schneider Trophy event. With only nine months in which to prepare for the race he decided to modify and increase the potential of the R engine. The design team at West Wittering succeeded in increasing output to 2,783hp, which made the final form of the R engine some 21 per cent more powerful than it had been in 1929. Mitchell, working in conjunction with Rolls-Royce at West Wittering and Derby, proposed certain modifications which increased the efficiency of his S6, which became designated the S6B.

The 1931 Schneider Trophy event was held on Sunday 13 September amid controversy surrounding the French and Italian teams, which had withdrawn from the race. Debate concerned the British team which, it was said, was unwilling for the event to be postponed while the competing teams perfected aircraft and engines. As sole contender for the race, it was far from being a token flypast for the British team: not only did Flight Lieutenant J.N. Boothman succeed in completing the course of seven laps at an average speed of 340.08mph, but Flight Lieutenant George Stainforth also took the world speed record to 407.5mph.

The R engine achieved fame during land-speed record attempts when installed in Malcolm Campbell's *Bluebird*; it was also used by Captain Eyston in *Thunderbolt* and *Speed of the Wind*, and for the world water speed runs in Kaye Don's *Miss England III* and Campbell's *Bluebird II* and *III*.

Sir Henry Royce was too ill to be able to watch the 1931 race. Instead he listened to the roar of the engine from his bed, and it is said that he was able to time the winning flight from the tone of the S6B's engine alone.

In addition to winning the Schneider Trophy for Britain, 1931 was the year that Rolls-Royce acquired the famous name of Bentley, the champion of Brooklands, Montlhéry and Le Mans. The acquisition of Bentley was not without controversy, and indeed the business dealings led to W.O. Bentley expressing much bitterness about the affair in his autobiography.

The Death of Sir Henry Royce

Sir Henry Royce died at his home at Elmstead, West Wittering, on 22 April 1933, shortly after his 70th birthday. Before his death he had agreed to the development of a new aero-engine which, incorporating many of the R's features, was designed as an altogether smaller unit, having a comparative performance that would be attractive for use in military aircraft. Designated PV12, the design emerged as the famous Merlin.

Royce had also agreed to the development of a new motor-car engine, which owed much of its design to aero-engine practice. Of V12 configuration and capacity of 7.3 litres, it was destined to power the Phantom III, which was introduced in 1936.

The Bentley as many remember it. This is KM3092, a 4-litre owned by Oliver Suffield. (Author's collection)

The Bentley Controversy

From its beginnings in 1919 Bentley Motors had led the way both on the race track and as fast and comfortable touring sports cars. Bentleys were a legend in their own lifetime, and there was hardly a schoolboy whose heroes did not include Tim Birkin and the Bentley Boys who had achieved so much for British

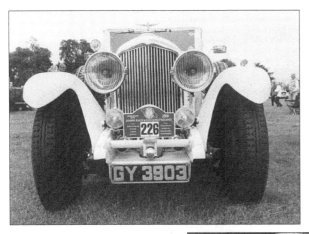

A Bentley 8-Litre owned by J.D. Medcalf and photographed in 2000. (Author's collection)

Right: Bentley Motors was acquired by Rolls-Royce in 1931 in what were viewed as controversial circumstances. W.O. Bentley was never happy with the arrangement and eventually left Rolls-Royce for Lagonda. Bentley was a fine engineer and designer, whose cars were synonymous with Brooklands and Le Mans. The name of Bentley became very closely associated with Rolls-Royce despite the two marques being separately marketed. (Courtesy Rolls-Royce & Bentley Motor Cars)

Bottom: W.O. Bentley with racing drivers John Duff and Frank Clement following their victory in 1924 at Le Mans. In the background can be seen A.F.C. Hillstead, who was part of the Bentley sales team. (Courtesy Rolls-Royce Motor Cars Limited)

motor racing. Many of the Bentley Boys were already household names: S.C.H. 'Sammy' Davis, Dr J.D. Benjafield, Glen Kidston, Clive and Jack Dunfee, Frank Clement, Bernard Rubin, Jean Chassagne, Dick Watney and Bertie Kensington-Moir. Bentley Motors was, however, under-capitalised from the outset, and for a long time had benefited from huge investment by one of the most famous of the Bentley Boys, the millionaire motor-racing driver Woolf Barnato.

There is no doubt that Bentley Motors lost out to the market that was dominated by relatively inexpensive mass-produced cars to the extent that a growing number of customers were reluctant to pay for hand-built luxury vehicles. For those customers who were prepared to pay for such luxury, and who wanted only the finest cars available, Bentley introduced the impressive 8-litre, which was designed to compete head-on with the Rolls-Royce Phantom II Continental. The Bentley was, in fact, a shade more expensive than the Derby product. The 8-litre was displayed at the 1930 London (Olympia) motor show, and Bentley directors were able to sell a considerable number of the cars.

Encouraging sales of the 8-litre were insufficient for the company to remain viable, and with some regret it was decided to introduce a model that would compete directly with the small Rolls-Royce. The result was the Bentley 4-litre which, in Bentley's words, was a car of unhappy memories. Using the 8-litre's chassis the car was underpowered and used a push-rod type engine, a recipe which the majority of Bentley customers found unpalatable. Despite this, the 4-litre was an excellent machine, and had it been marketed by any other company it would undoubtedly have attracted many buyers. With declining sales and mounting overheads, W.O. Bentley appealed to Woolf Barnato to invest once more in the Cricklewood company. However, Barnato had serious financial problems of his own and declined the invitation. Only one course of action was possible, and late in June 1931 a receiver was appointed.

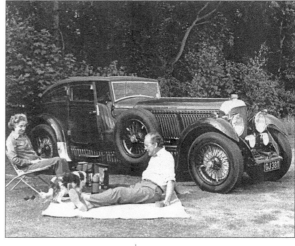

One of the most famous 'W.O.' Bentleys is HM2855, a 6-Litre originally owned by Woolf Barnato. While testing the car in France in 1930 he decided to race the renowned Blue Train from the south of France to London, reaching Pall Mall 3¹ hours ahead of it. The car is seen here in more recent years with Hugh Harben, a well-known Bentley enthusiast and past president of the Bentley Drivers Club. (Courtesy National Motor Museum)

For Bentley there remained a glimmer of hope. Only a matter of weeks after the receiver's appointment it became clear that Napier and Son Ltd of Acton were interested in acquiring Bentley Motors. Napier had been among the most respected of car makers, and having given up motor production six years earlier to concentrate all of their resources on aero-engines, the firm had decided to return to producing motor vehicles. The prospect of building luxury cars appealed strongly, even more so when Bentley was the designer. Negotiations had reached an advanced and significant stage by the end of July 1931 and Bentley was given leave to work with Napier on the design of a new model. In his autobiography, Bentley refers to the proposed car – the Napier-Bentley – as being an altogether more lithe machine than the 8-litre, which promised greater performance. There was a bonus, too, in that Napier was considering building a new aero-engine, and it was proposed that Bentley should design it.

In November 1931 the receiver applied for court approval of the Napier contract. No one at Napier, nor the receiver, had imagined that there might be a rival bid for Bentley Motors, and until the court was in session there had been no inkling that such a situation was possible. During the hearing, which was thought to be nothing more than a formality, a surprise offer for Bentley Motors was made from within the court. The offer was made as soon as Napiers' representative had stated the price, and was a fraction above that which had been disclosed. Following an adjournment, Napier increased its bid, which was immediately bettered by the unknown bidder representing the British Central Equitable Trust. It was at that point that the judge halted the hearing until later in the day, when sealed bids were to be opened. Napier was outbid by the smallest of margins, and for W.O. Bentley it was, he claimed, the most disastrous day of his life.

With the acquisition of Bentley Motors Rolls-Royce formed a new company, Bentley Motors (1931) Limited. A new car was designed that was built at Derby alongside Rolls-Royces. The new Derby-built Bentley proved popular despite much initial criticism and animosity among Bentley customers. Even W.O. Bentley acknowledged it to be a fine motor car. The first of the Derby Bentleys was the 3-litre, this particular example being owned by Oliver Suffield. (Courtesy Oliver Suffield)

Above: Known as the 'Silent Sportscar' the 3-litre Derby Bentley was designed with a 3,669cc engine that owed its origins to a shelved experimental Rolls-Royce project. (Courtesy Oliver Suffield)

Oliver Suffield parted with B21DK in 1965. Carrying the registration number MNC914, this 3-litre was originally registered as N63. Nightingale Road built 1,177 3-litre cars. (Courtesy Oliver Suffield)

Of the British Central Equitable Trust little or nothing was known. None of the syndicate's directors were identified, nor were any intentions for the future of Bentley revealed; the situation remained thus for several days. The identity of the mystery buyer was only exposed when W.O.'s wife returned from a cocktail party having overheard someone claiming that his company had acquired the old Bentley firm. That person was Arthur Sidgreaves, managing director of Rolls-Royce.

There is some evidence that negotiations were taking place regarding the future of Bentley before Bentley Motors went into liquidation. Woolf Barnato had, in effect, taken control of Bentley Motors and had appointed J.K. Carruth as managing director. It was Carruth who had contacted Arthur Sidgreaves proposing a possible merger, a move that the Rolls-Royce board had dismissed on the grounds that they were reluctant to take over a company that had not gone into liquidation, with liabilities that were not clearly defined. There was, however, the issue regarding Napier, and it is probable that Rolls-Royce, having previously rivalled the Acton firm in respect of motor cars, and more latterly aero-engines, was concerned that a Napier-Bentley agreement might jeopardise their market position.

When Rolls-Royce officially gained control of Bentley Motors in 1931 it formed a new company, Bentley Motors (1931) Ltd. Subsequent cars became known as 'Derby Bentleys' to distinguish them from the Cricklewood cars. An interesting point is that although Bentley was wholly owned by Rolls-Royce, nowhere on the cars or the owner handbooks did the name Rolls-Royce appear. The situation remained throughout the post-war years, even though Bentleys by that time were built at Crewe. It goes without saying that Bentley owners and enthusiasts are fiercely loyal to the marque, and there remains to this day a certain element within the Bentley fraternity which recognises neither the Derby nor the Crewe cars.

With the acquisition of Bentley, Rolls-Royce faced something of a dilemma. The company already had its range of 'smaller' cars as opposed to the Phantoms, which meant that there was some direct competition within the company itself. For some time Rolls-Royce directors did little or nothing about

the Bentley's Cricklewood works, which had come to a standstill: there was no reason to maintain production of the 8-litre, and there was little incentive to continue with the four-cylinder car. As for Bentley's stopgap 4-litre, sales had been disappointing, something which W.O. Bentley had envisaged.

The Bentley marque was

in danger of falling into obscurity unless something was done to profile the name. Rolls-Royce at least recognised the value and prestige associated with Bentley, and Ernest Hives decided that the experimental department at Nightingale Road should commence work on a 'new' Bentley. The economic climate had provoked Rolls-Royce into investigating development of a car, the Peregrine, that was smaller than the 20/25, but it had abandoned the programme because too few cost savings could be realised. By resurrecting Peregrine development and installing a 20/25hp engine modified from the original 2^i litres to give a capacity of 3,669cc,

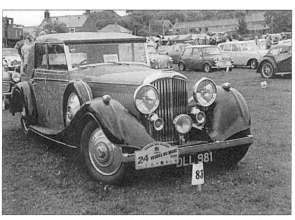

Hives foresaw the potential of such a car that would be built as a Bentley rather than a Rolls-Royce. There was no reason for continuing the Cricklewood operation, and the new Bentley would be built at Derby alongside Rolls-Royces. The car adopted the nomenclature 'The Silent Sportscar' which was associated with the model throughout the Derby era.

The emergence of the 3-litre was not without some controversy within Rolls-Royce itself. Royce believed that the new Bentley sports car could be designed using existing Rolls-Royce units, something to which Ernest Hives was opposed. As it happened Royce conceded that Hives had been correct in his belief that an entirely new car was preferential, and that the Derby Bentley was one of the nicest cars the company had built.

In similar fashion to Rolls-Royce motor cars and to Cricklewood Bentleys, Derby Bentleys were supplied to coachbuilders as a chassis only, and therefore a diversity of body styles courtesy of a wealth of coachwork specialists is found. The first of the Derby Bentley models was the 3-litre that was introduced in the autumn of 1933, a few months after the death of Sir Henry Royce. The new Bentley was well received, and it did attract a discerning clientele, even if 'W.O.' enthusiasts were aggrieved by its presence. Even W.O. Bentley offered his praise for the car; having been denied a place on the design team he was nevertheless very much involved in its testing and development, and after returning from France, during which time he was able to put the car thoroughly through its

paces, he wrote of it that he would rather own this Bentley than any other car produced under that name.

Ivan Evernden worked closely with coachbuilders Park Ward, the company having produced body-work for Rolls-Royce from 1920 and Bentley from 1924, and was responsible for designing the coachwork fitted to early 3-litre cars carrying

The 4-litre Derby Bentley was introduced in 1936 and the larger engine was at once applauded for its increase in power and smooth performance. The 4-litre chassis was fitted with a variety of coachwork styles, including this rare four-door tourer by Vanden Plas on chassis B12JD. The owner of this car, Douglas Trotter, insists on using the car to its full potential and is a regular competitor in Bentley Driver Club events in Britain and Europe. (Author's collection)

This fine 1937 4-litre (chassis B102LS) is owned by R.A. Burn. (Author's collection)

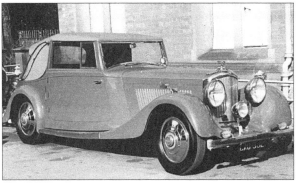

These two photographs of the Derby Bentley 4-litre (chassis B176GA), show the car with the hood lowered and raised, illustrating the vehicle's fine design. Despite the Derby Bentley being built alongside the Rolls-Royce, the cars were surprisingly different in both character and performance. Nowhere on the Bentley was there any mention of Rolls-Royce, and even the driver's handbook remained completely anonymous. (Courtesy Oliver Suffield)

that firm's coachwork. Park Ward produced more bodies for Derby Bentleys than any other coachbuilder, a situation no doubt brought about by the fact that in 1933 Rolls-Royce bought a minority stake in the business. In 1939 Park Ward became a wholly-owned subsidiary of Rolls-Royce, the latter having acquired the remaining shares.

In 1936 the 3-litre was superseded by the 4-litre, which offered improved performance. The specification of heavier coachwork as well as advancing technology had called for the increase in power, and the result was a car of extreme smoothness. Modifications were made to specification during the span of production, and in 1938 an overdrive gearbox was made available, along with a lower-ratio rear axle. At the time of the 4-litre's introduction W.O. Bentley had left Rolls-Royce to join Lagonda, remaining with that company until after World War Two.

Of all the 4-litre cars possibly the most famous is B27LE, a superbly aerodynamic machine designed by Frenchman Georges Paulin and built by the French coachbuilder Vanvooren. The car was supplied to the Greek racing driver A.M. Embiricos, and under test achieved some spectacular results, not least when Captain Eyston completed 114.63 miles in one hour at Brooklands, averaging 112mph.

The final chapter in the history of the Derby Bentley involves the Mk V, which was the product of a rationalisation policy within Rolls-Royce. The car was destined for a long career when the outbreak of war in 1939 halted construction after only nine production cars had been delivered. The Mk V Bentley had set the die for post-war production, and although the first of the Crewe cars shared a number of similarities to it, they were nevertheless quite different. The Mk V was also the basis for a proposed high performance sports saloon, again built by Vanvooren of Paris, which adopted the name Corniche. A machine of outstanding design, it incorporated advanced styling themes, the four-door coachwork displaying superb aerodynamics and featuring a cowled front end with faired-in headlamps. Georges Paulin was the architect, with some input from Ivan Evernden, and Vanvooren built the coachwork, which was constructed to afford the most stringent weight savings. The metal was made to a thinner gauge than that usually used, along with magnesium alloy castings. Vehicle 14-B-V was undergoing endurance testing in France when it was involved in a disastrous accident. The chassis was returned to Derby but the body, which was repaired at Chateauroux, was destroyed on the quayside at Dieppe while waiting to be shipped to England. The Corniche project was abandoned, but in the early post-war years was resumed, the development resulting in the introduction of the Bentley R-Type Continental.

Total Derby Bentley production accounted for 2,424 cars. Today, surviving examples are revered as keenly as the Cricklewood 'W.O.' models and are sought by loyal and discerning enthusiasts throughout the world.

Rolls-Royce without Sir Henry

After the death of Sir Henry Royce the design studio at West Wittering was closed, and the team that had worked there for so long was transferred to Nightingale Road under A.G. Elliott who, as senior engine designer, was appointed chief engineer. The team that relocated to Nightingale Road was thus: A.J. Rowledge (assistant chief engineer), C.L. Jenner (engine designer), Donald Eyre (engine draughtsman), Bernard Day (chassis, suspension, axles and brakes engineer), H.I.F. Evernden (exhausts systems, body mountings and coachwork engineer) and W.G. Hardy (transmissions engineer). Arthur Wormald remained as a director of the company as well its general works man-

ager, and he guided Rolls-Royce through what was a very difficult period in the company's history.

Wormald's health was failing, a fact that resulted in there being much uncertainty within Rolls-Royce, especially at Nightingale Road where morale became noticeably low. When Arthur

Nightingale Road as seen in 1937–8. Nearest the camera is the Rolls-Royce 25/30hp, the successor to the 20/25hp; behind are a couple of Bentley 4-litres. Notice the order of the assembly area, which is again devoid of activity. (Courtesy Sir Henry Royce Memorial Foundation)

Rolls-Royce Eagle and 20/25hp engines were used in a number of tank installations, and in this case a Cavalier A9 tank is fitted with the Phantom II engine. (Courtesy Bovington Tank Museum)

The Phantom III with its V12 engine represented the pinnacle of chassis production at Nightingale Road. The scene is of the Lord Mayor of Derby's visit to the works in 1937. By that time of course there was frenetic activity rebuilding Britain's arsenal in case of war. The 7.3-litre V12 engine was the last that Royce designed. (Courtesy Sir Henry Royce Memorial Foundation)

Phantom III engines being manufactured at Nightingale Road. These and all other engines were built to the tightest of tolerances and within Rolls-Royce practices were continually checked for quality. The Phantom V12 engines owed much of their design to aero-engine practice, and as for the chassis itself this proved to be arguably the most complicated of all that were built at Nightingale Road. (Courtesy Sir Henry Royce Memorial Foundation)

Wormald died in 1936 it had been expected that Harry Swift, the production manager, would take over as general works manager, but in the event he failed to do so. Harry Swift had joined Rolls-Royce in 1908, and in 1918 was appointed assistant works manger at Derby, retaining the post until 1928 when he was promoted to works manager. It was Ernest Hives who was appointed director and general works manager instead of Swift, and he at once began to restructure the working practices that had changed little since 1908.

At various times during the company's history there had been intense soul-searching about the market that Rolls-Royce should be in. Traditionally Rolls-Royce had supplied motor vehicles in the class which Hives referred to as the 'super expensive', and he argued for entering the moderate price car market as and when Rolls-Royce were in a position to produce cars at a more economical price. Hives was critical of some of the procedures within Rolls-Royce, and anticipated change and reorganisation. The Rolls-Royce board was confident that the new general manager could lead the company forward into a new era, and thus allowed him a free hand.

Before Ernest Hives was appointed director and general works manager, the tasks of building motor cars and aero-engines had been largely combined. Hives changed that. In July 1937 he divided Nightingale Road effectively into two distinct resources, the chassis division with R.W.

Among the last of the motor cars built at Nightingale Road was the 25/30hp Wraith. When this photograph was taken, itself an idyllic scene, war clouds were looming. The Merlin aero-engine was in production and measures were being taken to abandon car production in favour of aero-engines should war be declared. (Courtesy Rolls-Royce & Bentley Motor Cars Ltd)

Harvey-Bailey at the helm, and the aero division under the direction of A.G. Elliott. Harvey-Bailey's assistant was Roy Robotham, and Harry Swift was appointed under Elliott.

In early October 1935 Rolls-Royce announced the Phantom III, successor to the Phantom II and the last of the 40/50hp cars. The Phantom III's V12 engine owed much to aero-engine design, and had won the approval of Sir Henry Royce a short time before his death. The car was developed in accordance with growing competition from V8 and V12 engines, which were favoured by some European and American car makers, and was intended as a meaningful replacement for the Phantom II, which was perceived as outdated both in appearance and technology. When it was introduced at Olympia in the autumn of 1935, the Phantom III was arguably the most advanced production chassis then available. Its features included a 7,338cc overhead valve engine with a one-piece aluminium-alloy crankcase and cylinder blocks, cast-iron wet cylinder liners and an aluminium head.

Other features of the Phantom III chassis were independent front suspension of wishbone type with helical springs and hydraulic dampers; rear suspension

This is one of the best known of all Derby Bentleys. B27LE was built on the 4-litre chassis for the racing driver Nicky Embericos. With coachwork by Pourtout of Paris this is the car that achieved 115.05mph with Capt. George Eyston at the wheel. B27LE is pictured in post-war days. (Courtesy National Motor Museum)

B27LE photographed at Le Mans in 1951. The car was then owned by Michael Hay. Exactly what is happening in front of the car in the bottom picture is not entirely clear! The concept of this car, together with the experimental Corniche, paved the way for the post-war Bentley Continentals. (Courtesy National Motor Museum)

comprising semi-elliptic springs, a torsional stabiliser and automatic lubrication. The shock absorbers were adjustable to suit different travelling conditions and road surfaces, and were controlled by a device on the steering wheel. The chassis incorporated a hydraulic jacking system that was fitted to the front suspension and the rear axle to afford independent or combined operation, a hand pump being located beneath the front passenger's seat. Certainly the most complex Rolls-Royce model to that date, and one that required careful maintenance, the car attracted a particularly discerning clientele. It is not surprising therefore to discover that the Phantom III was the choice of members of the British royal family, although Daimler was the officially favoured marque. Woolf Barnato owned an example, as did Tommy Sopwith, H.O. Short and Hubert Scott-Paine of Supermarine. There is some conjecture about the exact number of Phantom IIIs that were built, but according to Nick Whitaker and Steve Stuckey who painstakingly researched the chassis records, the figure stands at 727.

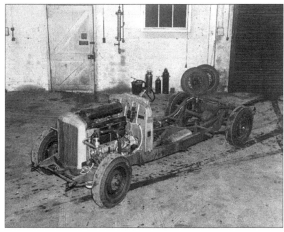

A year after the Phantom III was introduced, Rolls-Royce made available the 25/30hp chassis to supplant the 20/25hp. It was a modification of the 4-litre engine fitted to the 4-Derby Bentley that was used to power the 25/30, said by many marque enthusiasts to be one of the most enjoyable Rolls-Royces to drive. Having a wheelbase three inches longer than its predecessor, the car was fitted with a greater number of propriety parts than would have been evident had Royce been chief engineer. The change in policy was largely due to Roy Robotham's philosophy that component manufacturers were better placed for development than chassis manufacturers, who were free to concentrate on the wider issue of design. In Rolls-Royce tradition all of the 1,201 25/30s carried bespoke coachwork, Hooper producing the majority of bodies (209), wth Thrupp & Maberly building 207 and Park Ward 162.

The last of the Derby Rolls-Royces, the Wraith, was announced in 1938 as a smaller but companion model to the Phantom III. A number of the latter's features were to be found on the Wraith, such as a light alloy engine and independent front suspension. Some grand plans for the Wraith were discussed behind closed doors at Nightingale Road, much as proposals for a small V12 engine had once existed. A straight-eight engine had also been considered, but ultimately it was the six-cylinder 4-litre that was adopted. In total 492 Wraiths were built, 140 having coachwork by Park Ward.

Roy Robotham's rationalisation policy had been responsible for retaining the 4-litre engine and not progressing with other ideas. The economic climate meant that something had to be done about minimising the number of chassis types Rolls-Royce were employing, and to use, where possible, common components. Robotham noted the trend in the American motor industry and saw that the decline in bespoke coachbuilding would lead to very different manufacturing methods in the foreseeable future. He was right of course, as coachbuilding in Britain at the end of the 1930s was a mere shadow of what it had been, and after World War Two there were even fewer players. When Robotham had suggested that Rolls-Royce adopt standard body shells, which apart from any cost

Rolls-Royce planned to introduce a lightweight sports saloon in the full Bentley tradition for 1940. It was to have been known as the Corniche. The frame was based on the forthcoming Bentley Mk V 4-litre chassis, an example of which is seen here at Nightingale Road. (Courtesy Rolls-Royce & Bentley Motor Cars Ltd)

The Bentley Corniche existed only as an experimental car built at Nightingale Road on chassis 14-B-V. Designed as a Continental variant of the Bentley Mk V, the coachwork was designed by Georges Paulin and built in France by Vanvooren at Courbevoie, Seine. The car was tested in France and suffered a severe accident when the driver, Percy Rose, tried to avoid a car that had pulled out of a farm entrance ahead of him. The Corniche skidded on the wet road and hit a tree before coming to a halt in a ditch. The chassis was removed from the car and returned to Derby while the body was repaired in France. It was while the body was standing at Dieppe waiting to be shipped to England that it was destroyed by enemy bombing. In post-war years the concept of the car was revived with the introduction of the Bentley R-Type Continental. (Courtesy Rolls-Royce & Bentley Motor Cars Ltd)

The last production car to be built at Nightingale Road was the Bentley Mk V. Only a handful of the cars were produced before the outbreak of war halted chassis production. The model was the brainchild of Roy Robotham who, working with Hives's agreement, introduced a practice of chassis rationalisation in order to economise on components and costs. The bodies were built to a standard design because Robotham rightly anticipated a decline in bespoke coachbuilding. (Courtesy Rolls-Royce & Bentley Motor Cars Ltd)

saving ensured that consistent quality was maintained, he found himself at odds with some other senior managers. In accepting Robotham's philosophy both Ernest Hives and Harvey-Bailey adeptly provided for the future. During the final days of motor-car production at Nightingale Road, Roy Robotham's rationalisation policy was instrumental in the introduction of the Bentley Mark V and the Wraith.

Around the time of Sir Henry Royce's death the familiar red R-R emblem on a Rolls-Royce's radiator was changed to black. There is absolutely no evidence that this was done to mourn Sir Henry. Coachbuilders had petitioned Rolls-Royce to have the emblem changed in colour, and Royce had approved the alteration before his death.

Within the aero division, there was, during the mid-1930s, huge activity supplying and re-arming the armed forces. This pushed through development of the Merlin engine, and later led to the production of aero-engines for the war effort.

CHAPTER SIX

THE MERLIN AND GRIFFON

IN THE MID-1930s Germany's re-armament and military expansion provoked Stanley Baldwin's Conservative government to look closely at Britain's defence resources. What emerged from the inquiry was that the aircraft industry seemed to be lacking both equipment and personnel, and was certainly in no position to adequately defend the nation. Some 35,000 people were at the time employed in aircraft manufacturing, 20 per cent of them being employed by Rolls-Royce.

A massive programme of equipping the armed forces was clearly necessary, and much of the burden fell to the aircraft manufacturing industry fabricating airframes, components and aero-engines. The task was enormous and in the spring of 1936 the government approached the motor industry to help build for the future. The proposal was that 'shadow factories' would help supply the aero industry with materials, and meetings were hurriedly arranged with Austin, Daimler, Rover, Standard and Rootes. The plan was that car-makers were to act as manufacturing agents and receive payment on an agreed basis for work completed. Furthermore each manufacturer was given some choice about the factory's location. The Air Ministry remained responsible for factory building costs and met the required amounts of capital, as well as agreeing to pay annual management fees of £50,000. Additionally it was agreed that the Air Ministry would contribute £75 for every aero-engine that was built.

Negotiations were at first protracted, as some car manufacturers were opposed to the scheme, and it was only when Rootes agreed an arrangement that the other manufacturers responded. From then on the planning of shadow factories progressed quickly and construction work began on the first shadow factory at Longbridge, the Austin works near Birmingham, in May 1936. Within weeks other factories were in the process of being built. As the international crisis deepened it became apparent that the shadow factories in operation had insufficient capacity to fully provide for the demands of war, and therefore a second wave of factories was planned. It was to Rolls-Royce that the

The Merlin engine was derived from a project that began in October 1932 to develop a more powerful aero-engine than had previously been built. This was a private venture arrangement, PV12, which had, in effect, evolved from the development of the Kestrel engine. The latter is shown in this photograph which shows Ernest Hives (on the extreme left) with Arthur Sidgreaves (centre), Arthur Wormald and (far right) A.J. Lidsey. The latter joined Rolls-Royce as a development technical assistant and retired in the 1950s. Lidsey married Arthur Wormald's daughter. When the design of the PV12 was first conceived the RAF was sadly lacking in modern aircraft and equipment. (Courtesy Sir Henry Royce Memorial Foundation)

government appealed for assistance. From the outset of the shadow factory scheme, Rolls-Royce was reluctant to agree to any arrangement whereby production of its engines would be undertaken by any other manufacturer. Rather than build a new factory, discussions with the company resulted in the extension of the production area of Nightingale Road by some 311,540 square feet. In the event it was evident that the restructured Derby works still lacked sufficient capacity to fulfil its aero-engine orders.

The problems regarding aero-engine production ultimately led to Ernest Hives agreeing to the building of two shadow factories, one at Merrill's Farm, Crewe, and the other at Hillington near Glasgow. An interesting aside is that in 1935 Hives had been a guest at Heinkel's factory in Germany, where he discovered that some 600 research technicians were busy developing aero equipment, the number being equal to the combined technical workforce at Rolls-Royce, Armstrong-Whitworth, Blackburn, Fairey, Hawker, Gloster and Supermarine.

As building for the war effort intensified, Ernest Hives and his colleagues conceded that the chassis division, which had spare capacity, would have to surrender some of its area to aero-engine production. So vital was it to fulfil orders that there had at one time been a proposal to move chassis production away from Nightingale Road, to premises at Burton upon Trent, which were earmarked for the purpose. As it happened events overtook any such planning; aero-engine production commenced at Crewe, and with the prospect of war ever more likely, Hives made contingency plans involving car building being halted.

When war was declared on 3 September 1939, all car making at Nightingale Road effectively stopped. Tooling, patterns and car manufacturing equipment was rapidly dismantled, experimental cars were removed and chassis division personnel were instructed to store everything in secure accommodation wherever it could be found locally. Mindful that when the war was over there would be a return to car making, Roy Robotham collected two complete sets of blueprints of car designs then under development and had one shipped to Canada for safe-keeping throughout the duration of hostilities. Two experimental cars were also sent to Canada (one of which remains in service), and the second set of blueprints were secured in a bank vault in the nearby town of Ashby-de-la-Zouch.

The Air Ministry had demanded that in the event of war there should be maximum dispersal of executive and technical personnel. Bill Allen, who was working under Ivan Evernden, recalled that lorries arrived at the factory and were loaded with all the drawing office equipment, which was transported to Blount's Hosiery Mill in Penn Street, Belper, where the draughtsmen were relocated.

While the majority of fitters were transferred from the chassis division to the aero division, there remained work to do for chassis division engineers, not only in respect of motor vehicles, but also in armaments, aero-engines and tanks. Hives preoccupied himself with aero-engines and based himself in the now-empty executive offices at Nightingale Road. Roy Robotham was detailed to move his department into alternative premises, a task that was far from easy owing to the fact that suitable accommodation was virtually unavailable. Eventually premises were found at a disused iron foundry at Clan in Derbyshire. The foundry owners were delighted to negotiate a rent for the works which, apart from having thick dust covering every surface, were squalid and rat-infested. Once the place had been made habitable, and a concrete floor was laid over the earth surface, it formed the nucleus of the department until after the end of the war.

The chassis division did not return to Nightingale Road but instead was established at Crewe in the shadow factory that was converted from Merlin and Griffon aero-engine production. The Clan foundry not only contributed greatly to the war effort by supporting the Derby works in respect of technical development, but it also became the centre of research and design for the Meteor tank engine. In this work the chassis division excelled itself, under the guidance of Roy Robotham and Ivan Evernden.

PV12

To return to the development of the Merlin engine, experience with the Kestrel had dictated that a more powerful aero-engine was needed. Sir Henry Royce had sanctioned the engine's development as a private venture in October 1932, and work commenced on what was known as PV12 (PV for Private Venture) in January 1933. From the outset Royce had anticipated using as much technology as possible that had been gained from the R engine, which, he believed, would further the success that had already been demonstrated with the Kestrel. It is important to stress that the PV12 did not materialise from the R engine but rather the Kestrel. The R engine was directly instrumental in the emergence of the Griffon engine. Working closely with

Development of the Merlin engine took a little over three years, which was miraculous. The engine passed its 50-hour civil type-test at the end of 1935. A number of problems had beset Rolls-Royce engineers regarding the engine's development, and it was only through the determined efforts of Ernest Hives and his team that progress was made so quickly. This photograph shows Merlins under construction at Nightingale Road. (Courtesy Sir Henry Royce Memorial Foundation)

Royce on what became the Merlin project was A.G. Elliott, both, of course, accommodated at West Wittering. It is at this point pertinent to re-establish Rolls-Royce's policy of naming their aero-engines after birds of prey. For some people the Merlin was more associated with Merlin the Magician than any bird!

From their design studio at West Wittering, Royce and Elliott broadcast their ideas to Ernest Hives and his team of engineers at Nightingale Road, which comprised A.J. Rowledge, A.A. Rubbra, Cyril Lovesey and Jimmy Ellor.

Early design proposals had included building the engine in an 'upside-down' position so that when fitted in an aircraft's fuselage the wide 'V' of the cylinder banks would mean improved pilot visibility. Ultimately the principle was abandoned following discussions with airframe manufacturers Hawker and Supermarine. A similar principle was, however, used on both the Junkers and Daimler-Benz engines when fitted to the Messerschmitt BF109. How the design

Merlins under construction at Nightingale Road in the part of the factory that was known as the 'glass house'. At the outbreak of war in 1939 motor chassis production ceased immediately and all available space was given over to producing aero-engines. In the build up to war chassis assembly had already given over some of its space capacity to aero-engine building. During wartime the numbers of personnel at Nightingale Road were dramatically increased, and the Derby workforce accounted for some 20,000 employees. Twelve-hour shifts were in operation, employees working days one week and nights the other. It is recalled that the pressure to build engines was so great that everything was done to keep productivity going, even to the extent that workers sang well-known and popular songs in order to maintain a working rhythm. (Courtesy Sir Henry Royce Memorial Foundation)

of these engines materialised is a matter of some conjecture, but it is believed that soon after the design team became involved in the PV12, a party of German aero-engineers on a visit to Nightingale Road saw a mock-up of the already aborted layout outside Rowledge's office. It has been claimed that the design that Junkers and Daimler-Benz perpetuated did have certain disadvantages, which is why a system of direct fuel injection was formulated by the Germans, who were experienced in such technology.

Initial research and development took some nine months, and it was October 1933 before the first of two engines that were built was ready for testing. A number of problems were revealed, not least that bench testing showed there to be cracking of the cylinder jackets. The engine's double-helical reduction gears also proved troublesome, and in an attempt to overcome the problem straight-cut spur gears were substituted. While it appeared reasonably straightforward to resolve the latter difficulty, it was the former that required intense development to arrive at a suitable solution. The initial response was to strengthen the integral cylinder block and upper part of the crankcase, but this did not produce a reliable result. Ultimately, after trials using different types of cylinder head, it was decided that the only alternative was to redesign the engine using separate castings for the two components.

It was July 1934 when the PV12 was put through its 100-hour type-test which revealed it to provide 625hp at 2,500rpm for take-off, and 790hp at 12,000 feet. Despite the conclusive testing there was much further development, and when the engine was subjected to a 50-hour civil type-test in 1935, further problems were encountered.

The PV12 was first flown on 21 February 1935 when it was installed in a Hawker Hart biplane, K3036. The test pilot was Ronald Harker who, after the flight, claimed that the PV12-powered Hart was the fastest-climbing aircraft in Britain! Flight testing the PV12 was conducted for some 60 hours, much of that time being spent in evaluating the engine's cooling system.

Hucknall Plays its Part

For many years the installation of test engines remained the responsibility of aircraft manufacturers, and Rolls-Royce was often at the mercy of conditions beyond its control. Therefore, when problems arose, it was the engine that was blamed for failure when in fact that was usually not the case. Ernest Hives had made a study of these failures and arrived at the conclusion that most problems were caused by faulty installation. In addition to manufacturer testing, the Royal Aircraft Establishment at Farnborough undertook flight testing, which produced some important and revealing information. Owing to the vagaries of flight testing over which Rolls-Royce had little or no control, the company established its own flight-testing establishment in 1934 at Hucknall RAF aerodrome near Nottingham.

Operations at Hucknall were preceded by the establishment of a department at Nightingale Road to study the problems and issues surrounding the installation of Rolls-Royce engines. Cyril Lovesey was involved in this from the very beginning, and three years later in 1932 helped form a small department

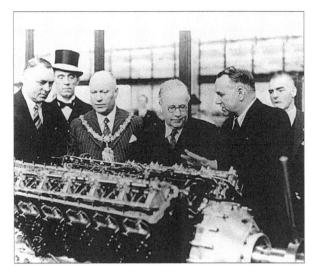

Ernest Hives explains the workings of the Merlin engine to Sir Kingsley Wood, the Air Minister, in 1938. On the far left is John Morris, one of Nightingale Road's most experienced engineers, who was appointed manager of the new Rolls-Royce factory at Crewe. The photograph was taken during the opening ceremony of the Crewe works; Harry Bricker, mayor of Crewe, is standing between John Morris and Sir Kingsley Wood. (Courtesy Rolls-Royce & Bentley Motor Cars Ltd)

based at Tollerton airfield, also near to Nottingham, which was operated by the Nottingham Flying Club. Two aircraft were allocated to aero-engine development under Lovesey's watchful eye, a Hawker Horsley which was fitted with a Buzzard engine, and a Fairey IIIF fitted with a Kestrel. The Nottingham club's chief instructor, Captain Ronnie Shepherd, did the test flying.

When Rolls-Royce established the Hucknall flight-testing department Captain Shepherd was appointed chief test pilot. His assistant was Ronald Harker, who was already based at the airfield, flying with the Auxiliary 504 Squadron. Two further engineers completed the small but select team: engine tester Harold Green and rigger Frank Purnell. As more aircraft arrived, including the aforementioned Hawker Hart, so the Hucknall enterprise expanded. A drawing office was established, then came a machine shop and sheet metal and coppersmiths, together with a propeller test bed and, importantly, a wind tunnel.

The Hucknall flight-testing establishment proved to be a most valuable asset to Rolls-Royce. The company purchased a Heinkel He70 for experimental purposes, the aircraft being renowned for its clean lines and low drag factor. When ordering the aeroplane Rolls-Royce had sent a Kestrel engine to Germany to be installed in it. When the aircraft was delivered it was discovered that the Kestrel had been test-flown in a Messerschmitt 109 for almost 60 hours before having been installed in the Heinkel. Cyril Lovesey appointed Ray Dorey as manager at Hucknall, a wise decision, since Dorey had been deputy chief tester under Lovesey throughout the R engine programme. Ronald Harker recalled those heady days at Hucknall when Dorey's philosophy was to 'work until it hurts', something that Sir Henry Royce would no doubt have approved.

At Nightingale Road, development of the PV12 was being undertaken at a break-neck rate, although it probably did not appear like that at the time. In customary fashion engines were built, tested and dismantled, each time careful note being taken of their condition. The 50-hour civil type-test was eventually completed in December 1935 when 955bhp at 2,600rpm was recorded at 11,000 feet. Maximum output was established to be 1,045bhp at 3,000rpm at 12,000 feet. From then on the PV12 became known as the Merlin, and arrangements were put in hand to begin production of Merlin I.

The fact that Merlin development took a mere 38 months from its inception is remarkable. Much of the success must be due to the fact that Rolls-Royce as a whole, and Royce, Elliott, Hives and their dedicated teams in particular, had gained considerable experience from work carried out for the Schneider Trophy programme. That the Merlin became synonymous with the Battle of Britain is tribute to the fact that the engine had a specific role powering a new generation of aircraft – not the biplanes that had been largely used for testing purposes, but streamlined monoplanes.

For Ernest Hives and his team at Nightingale Road the route to perfecting the Merlin engine had been what he referred to as a nightmare. The factory had three other aero-engines under development at the same time as the Merlin: the

Vulture, Peregrine and the Exe, the latter being the first Rolls-Royce engine not to be named after a bird of prey.

The final weeks of 1935 were a turning point in the career of the Merlin for a reason other than the fact that the engine had passed its 50-hour civil type-test. It was the time that the government accepted that something had to be done urgently to provide the RAF with an effective and powerful front-line fighting machine. That meant new aeroplanes, and aero-engines to power them. Arriving at that decision had been a convoluted process with arguments and counter-arguments relating to the RAF's requirements. Ultimately Air Marshall Sir Hugh Dowding won the challenge, and it was through his efforts that the Air Ministry specified in 1930 that a day and night fighter – a 'killer fighter' – was needed to replace existing outdated machines. The specification, F7/30, was all-important: such an aircraft should have a low landing speed and low landing run, a maximum speed of 250mph, a steep initial climb rate to enable interception, high manoeuvrability, good all-round view and four Vickers machine guns as weaponry. The brief did not suggest any particular style of airframe, but clearly the need was for a clean, low-drag shape.

Six aircraft manufacturers submitted their designs in respect of specification F7/30, among which were Supermarine and Hawker. That the Spitfire and Hurricane emerged from the exercise is well known, even if R.J. Mitchell's Type 224 monoplane was, according to Gordon Mitchell (R.J.'s son), a near disaster. Mitchell acknowledged that his Type 224 was a mistake, and he set about, with Supermarine chairman Sir Robert McLean's full authority, designing a new and better aeroplane. Type 224, named 'Spitfire' by McLean, had been powered by a 600hp steam-cooled Goshawk II engine, which in this particular installation, had presented some cooling difficulties, and the aeroplane's speed at 230mph fell short of what had been expected.

Merlin and the Spitfire

The design that emerged from Mitchell's efforts was completely different from that of Type 224. Type 300, as it was referred to, had some unique features. Still known as Spitfire, Mitchell's design diverted from the then current belief that high-lift thick wings were appropriate, and instead included a wing that was relatively thin but which had sufficient strength to accommodate machine guns and a retractable undercarriage. The shape of the wing was unusual as it was of elliptical plan form. Mitchell's design team had worked hard on the aircraft's streamlining, and the drag coefficient, which was largely to blame for the Type 224's failure, was greatly reduced thanks to Joe Smith, Supermarine's chief draughtsman and Mitchell's deputy.

It was not only with aerodynamics that Mitchell was concerned. Rolls-Royce's development of the PV12 suggested it to have far better performance than the Goshawk had provided, and that its testing at Hucknall had shown that a change from steam to pure ethylene glycol as a means of cooling was beneficial, changed the course of history. The Merlin engine was thus adopted for use in the Spitfire.

Some important issues arose from the development of the Merlin and Spitfire. The finance for building the prototype Spitfire, Supermarine's fighter K5054, was partly provided by a donation of £7,500 from Rolls-Royce, then a

considerable sum. R.J. Mitchell's work on the Spitfire was conducted at a time when the designer was seriously ill with bowel cancer. Mitchell saw the Spitfire take its maiden flight with Vickers chief test pilot Captain 'Mutt' Summers at the controls on the afternoon of the 5 March 1936; then on 11 June 1937 he died, leaving Britain and the aero industry a legacy that will never be forgotten.

Captain Mutt Summers was obviously impressed by the Spitfire's performance. Climbing out of the cockpit he told Mitchell 'I don't want anything changed'. That, of course, did not preclude continuation of technical development.

Intense work on the Merlin was progressing at Nightingale Road with the appointment of two engineers who helped shape the future of Rolls-Royce's business. One was Colonel Tim Barrington, who had in fact resigned from the company in 1921 having intimated to the Air Ministry that Rolls-Royce's future lay not with aero-engines. Barrington had then worked for Bentley, and when the firm was acquired by Rolls-Royce he joined Bristol aero-engines under Roy Fedden. When he rejoined Rolls-Royce in 1934, Barrington was appointed chief designer and remained at Derby until the outbreak of World War Two when he was appointed, along with Jimmy Ellor, to the Ministry of Aircraft Production. Ellor and Barrington were posted to Packard to assist with Merlin production in America, but it was while he was in the US that Barrington died.

Dr Stanley Hooker, later Sir Stanley, joined Rolls-Royce at Nightingale Road in January 1938 having sought a career at the Woolwich Arsenal where he specialised in aerodynamics, anti-aircraft rockets and supercharging. Ernest Hives was already aware of Stanley Hooker's abilities as a brilliant mathematician, and possibly his interview at Nightingale Road was no more than a formality. Lacking practical experience, Hooker was detailed to produce a paper on supercharging, something which Jimmy Ellor knew all about. Ellor was so impressed with the paper and the author's ability that he immediately arranged for Hooker's appointment as assistant experimental chief engineer. As such, the appointment called for special responsibilities regarding the development of superchargers.

More Merlins

Merlin I development led to the introduction of the Merlin II, which employed redesigned cylinder heads. Those of the Merlin I were of the detachable ramp type, while the Merlin II's were cast in unit with the blocks, thus reverting to earlier aero-engine design practice. When *Flight* magazine published details of the two engines it emerged that in excess of 2,000 flying hours had been completed and that the engines showed a marked superiority over the Kestrel. Merlin II development heralded the Merlin III, which provided phenomenal performance owing to modifications relating to the airscrew shaft, strengthened pistons and connecting rods.

Merlin IIs and IIIs were fitted to the Spitfire I, Defiant I, Hurricane and Sea Hurricane Is together with the Battle I, aircraft that were the front line fighting force in the Battle of Britain, the 1940 theatre of war that has been compared to the significance of the Battle of Trafalgar of 1805. It was Lord Tedder, Marshal of the Royal Air Force, who claimed that Britain owed its victory in 1940 to three factors, the pilots' skill and bravery, the Rolls-Royce Merlin engine, and the availability of suitable fuel.

Derby engineers Roy Robotham, Harry Grylls, John Reid and John Blatchley, all of whom served at the Clan foundry, are pictured in later years at a Clan foundry reunion. (Courtesy John Blatchley)

The Merlin IV was introduced with pressure-water cooling in place of glycol cooling, the engine having been primarily developed for the Armstrong-Whitworth Whitley bomber. Then came the Mk VIII, a medium-supercharged unit rated at 1,010hp at 2,850rpm at 6,750ft. When it used 100-octane fuel, the Merlin VIII delivered 1,080hp at 3,000rpm for take-off. Merlin Xs were used to power the Halifax I, Wellington II and Whitley V and VII bombers, and as such represented a breakthrough in design. The engine featured a two-speed supercharger that gave improved fuel economy under cruising conditions and more power at take-off.

When the Spitfire II was introduced, some aircraft were fitted with the Merlin XII with a Rotol three-blade constant-speed airscrew; the output of the engine, which featured a 0.477:1 reduction gear, was rated at 1,150hp (maximum) at 3,000rpm at 14,000ft. Rolls-Royce went on to develop the Merlin XX, which was intended to be interchangeable with the Merlin X. The XX was designed with a two-speed supercharger, which provided a marked increase in power to provide 1,240hp in low gear at 2,850rpm and, in high gear, 1,175hp at 2,850rpm. These figures alone accounted for some 250hp increase compared to the Merlin II. Despite the increase in power, the engineers at Nightingale Road had managed to keep the weight of the engine remarkably low, the dry weight having risen by only 75lbs. The aeroplanes that were fitted with Merlin XXs were the Beaufighter II, Defiant II, Halifax II and V, Hurricanes II and IV, and the Lancasters I and III.

Five more examples of the Merlin, 21, 22, 23, 24 and 25, shared similarities with the XX. Mosquitos I, II, III, IV and VI received the 21; the Lancaster I and II, along with the York I, were fitted with the 22; the 23 was installed in some of the aforementioned Mosquitos (except the III) together with the VII and VIII. Some Lancaster and York I's, as well as the Lancaster III, received the Merlin 24 while the Merlin 25 was offered to the Mosquitos VI and XIX.

Rolls-Royce produced in excess of 120 Merlin variants, some of which were built by Packard in America and others by the Ford Motor Company in Britain at Trafford Park, Manchester. The applications, rated to individual aircraft types, were enormously varied and extended to civil requirements once the war was over. The first of the civil Merlins was the Type 102, after which emerged the 500 series that was fitted to Lancastrian and York airliners, and the 600 series, which employed two-speed and two-stage supercharging. For the North Atlantic route the 620 was introduced specifically for the Canadair North Star DC4 airliners in operation with Trans Canada Airlines; further modifications included intercooling and charge heating. In addition to the Canadair airliners, Merlin application included Avro Tudor IIs, IVs, IVBs and Vs, and the Argonauts in use with BOAC. Merlins did not power aircraft exclusively, they were also fitted to marine craft, and when the engine was developed for tank installations it became known as the Meteor.

Mention has already been made of the Crewe shadow factory, which was built with urgent speed and began building Merlin engines in 1938. Nightingale Road personnel were responsible for the laying out of the factory for aero-engine production, and they were also instrumental in training the Crewe staff before assembly could commence. It was Jack Aitcheson, one of Nightingale Road's most highly skilled engineers, who was delegated to install a couple of

Merlin engines along with some machine tools at the premises of the Co-Operative Wholesale Society milk depot in Crewe before the factory at Merrill's Farm was ready for occupation. The first recruits arrived for duty on 8 August 1938, and it was under Aitcheson's watchful eye that they were subjected to rigorous training, stripping down the Merlins and rebuilding them until each was conversant with the engine's 19,000 components. By the end of 1938 there were over 400 people employed building Merlins at the Crewe shadow factory.

John Morris, a senior engineer at Nightingale Road, was appointed by Ernest Hives as Crewe's works manager. Under him were seven engineers, also from Nightingale Road. They were Jack Valentine, R.E. (Dick) Garner, Ron Dyson, Wilson Elliott, Bill Harvey and Walter Dutton, as well as the aforementioned Jack Aitcheson.

Merlins and Meteors

The chassis division personnel at the Clan foundry undertook development of the Merlin for use in tanks. British tanks at the outset of World War Two were lacking in capability and were expected to perform using engines that had been designed during World War One. Leyland had been given the task of developing a new tank, but the company was reliant on the Liberty aero-engine which was seriously outmoded by modern enemy equipment. Ernest Hives had directed Roy Robotham to devise a method of equipping Leyland with a reliable engine with a suitable power to weight ratio. The funding for the project came from the government, to the tune of £1 million.

Robotham would have preferred to embark upon the project without any preconceived ideas, but because time was of the essence there was no alternative but to modify an existing product. To have designed and developed a new engine would simply have taken too long. Realising that a Rolls-Royce aero-engine would be an eminently suitable replacement for the ageing Liberty, there remained the dilemma as to which to use, the Kestrel or the Merlin. Because it was not supercharged the Kestrel seemed the most appropriate, but it soon became apparent that it gave insufficient power. The Merlin was therefore the answer, not with its usual supercharger but fitted instead with a large twin-choke updraught SU carburettor and using pool petrol, a low-octane fuel used extensively for ground operations during the war. Rolls-Royce engineers worked in close co-operation with Leyland engineers, and because the Clan foundry was without any manufacturing or tooling facilities, drawings produced by Ivan Evernden and Bill Allen were rushed to the Leyland factory, where priority was given to engineering the components. However cumbersome the arrangement seemed, it nevertheless worked efficiently and

The Spitfire, one of the most famous aircraft of all time. Fitted with the Merlin engine, the Spitfire and Rolls-Royce are synonymous. Later versions of the aircraft were fitted with the Griffon engine. On its first test flight, Captain J. 'Mutt' Summers, Vickers' chief test pilot, had the task of taking the prototype Spitfire into the air. On landing after a successful flight it is recorded that Summers said that 'I don't want anything changed'. This was perceived by some to mean that the aeroplane was perfect. Although there were no major snags, Summers had in fact trimmed the aircraft to his requirements, and his comments indicated that there lay ahead many months of testing and alterations before the aeroplane could go into production. The Spitfire's maiden flight had been curtailed by overheating caused by over caution before take-off. Spitfires were prone to overheating during long taxiing and delays at the holding point; Summers, knowing the aircraft was going to perform well in flight, was keen to get airborne more sharply on the second flight to prevent the engine overheating, and was thus adamant that nothing be touched. (Courtesy Rolls-Royce & Bentley Motor Cars Ltd)

The Merlin lives on... This could have been a scene from wartime days but is in fact a more recent picture taken when preparing for an airshow. Merlins and Griffons were fitted to a wide range of aircraft both during and after World War Two. In addition to the Spitfire the Merlin was fitted to BOAC Argonauts and the 620 version saw service with Canadair North Star DC4 airliners on the North Atlantic operation. In addition to Spitfires the Griffon was fitted to the Avro Shackleton maritime-reconnaissance aircraft. (Author's collection)

the prototype engines were sent to Clan, where they were put on test under the supervision of Charlie Caisley. As a young apprentice, Reg Spencer could often be found sitting on top of test engines taking regular thermometer readings.

To everybody's relief the results proved satisfactory; basically because Robotham's team had devised an engine that was essentially a Merlin with the blower removed and which could develop 600bhp, the figure predicted to propel a 30-ton tank at speeds in excess of 25mph. The modified Merlin became known as the Meteor and proved highly successful when installed in the Crusader tank. On trial at Rolls-Royce's test track at Burley Hill, Quarndon, and particularly at the army's proving ground at Aldershot, Crusaders could be seen thundering along the standard ¹-mile speed course at speeds in excess of 50mph. This was at a time when the army's test team was used to seeing tanks crawling along at not much more than a snail's pace. Rolls-Royce was unpopular with Derbyshire's Highways Authority as tanks on test frequently lifted the catseyes out of the centre of the road when passing along the A6 through Belper.

Leyland and Rolls-Royce parted company over tank design. Leyland decided there were problems with the Meteor engine's cooling and returned to using the Liberty, which was used to propel the Centaur tank. Rolls-Royce struck up a partnership with the Birmingham Railway Carriage and Wagon Company to

Rolls-Royce saw many theatres of war. This 40/50hp Silver Ghost is pictured while in use with the Home Guard in the Brighton area. (Courtesy Sir Henry Royce Memorial Foundation)

develop a new heavy cruiser tank, the outcome of which was the Cromwell. Leyland's Centaur was a failure because of inherent engine problems and the company eventually took over Cromwell production. Another famous tank was the Leyland Comet, which was also was fitted with the Meteor engine. Rolls-Royce's contribution to tank design during World War Two was immeasurable, and went a long way towards ensuring an Allied victory.

The Griffon

The Rolls-Royce Griffon engine, which was to give the Spitfire a new lease of life, emerged as a direct result of the R engine. Arthur Rubbra recalled that the Griffon was a de-rated version of the R and was first tested in 1933. Further development was deferred until 1939 when it was realised that having a larger engine than the Merlin that would fit existing installations would be an advantage. The Griffon I, using the same bore and stroke measurements as the R, ran in the experimental department at Nightingale Road in November 1939, research having been based on the belief that such an engine would compete with advanced types of radial engines then under development. One particular application intended for the Griffon was use with the Fleet Air Arm's torpedo bombers, where high power at low altitudes was essential. The dimensions of the Merlin and Griffon were similar, the latter being only very slightly larger. Nevertheless the Griffon's swept volume was 35.9 per cent greater than that of the Merlin.

The detailed design of the Griffon was quite different to the Merlin in that the camshaft, magneto and supercharger drives were heavily modified and moved from the rear of the engine to the front. The method of lubrication, whereby main bearings and big ends were fed with oil from the hollow interior of the crankshaft, was also novel. The Griffon II was the first of the Griffons to go into production and was fitted to the

The British government awarded Rolls-Royce £1 million to develop the Meteor engine. The chassis division outposted at the Clan foundry was given charge of design and the aero division became responsible for production. The whole question of British tank reliability was raised when testing of the Meteor commenced, and as a result Rolls-Royce became involved in improving overall tank design. Meteors were fitted to Centurion tanks, as shown in this photograph. (Courtesy Bovington Tank Museum)

The development of the Merlin was a team effort but it certainly would not have materialised so quickly had it not been for Ernest Hives. Elevated to the peerage in 1950, Lord Hives is seen here at Derby on the occasion of his retirement in 1957. With him is Lady Hives, and on the right can be seen Dr Llewellyn Smith. (Courtesy Sir Henry Royce Memorial Foundation)

It was Ernest Hives's influence that led to the introduction of the Meteor tank engine. Leyland Motors had originally been given the task of devising a modern engine suitable for use with tanks and approached Rolls-Royce for assistance. Hives was not impressed by Leyland's plans and suggested that the Merlin be developed. The result was the Meteor, which was used to propel the Cromwell tank from 1942, an example of which is pictured here. (Courtesy Bovington Tank Museum)

Fairey Firefly. This, and Marks III and IV, had two-speed, single-stage blowers and gave maximum power of 1,720hp for take-off and 1,735hp at 16,000ft. Griffon IIIs and IVs were installed in the Spitfire XII and XIV as a means of combating the Focke-Wulf 190, Germany's most feared single-seat piston-engined fighter.

As with the Merlin, the Griffon became synonymous with the Spitfire. One of the more innovative applications was the Griffons 85, 87 and 88, which had a drive for contra-rotating airscrews, the engine appearing in the Spitfire XIV and 21 along with the Seafire 45 and 47. Contraprop Griffons also powered the Avro Shackleton maritime-reconnaissance aircraft which, for many years post-war, provided outstanding service, the aircraft finally being retired in 1991. Among the most remarkable of Griffon developments was the 101 series, which incorporated three-stage supercharging together with Rolls-Royce fuel injection.

In total some 150,000 Merlins were built, the output of Derby, Crewe and Glasgow averaging 1,800 per year. Early in the war Merlin production had been limited, and during the first year no more than 2,000 left the assembly lines. The 100,000th engine was delivered on 29 March 1944.

It is remarkable that the factories building the Merlin and Griffon engines escaped serious damage by the Luftwaffe. Certainly Crewe was bombed with the loss of 16 lives, and Trafford Park, Manchester, was bombed twice while the factory was under construction, thankfully with only one fatality. The Hillington works at Glasgow were the target of incendiary bombs which were extinguished before too much damage was done, but when a high-explosive bomb did hit the site one person was killed. Nightingale Road was attacked once, fortunately without extensive damage and without loss of life. Derby was frequently the target of attack by enemy aircraft, presumably because of the Rolls-Royce factory, which was heavily camouflaged and thus difficult to identify from the air. German propaganda had people believe that on one occasion the Rolls-Royce Derby factory had been wrecked with the loss of some

5,000 motorcycles! In truth Derby had been bombed, but on that particular occasion the bombs had missed the factory and fallen on market gardens, the only casualties being a field of tomatoes.

The Merlin and Griffon were responsible for a four-fold

Left: When Roy Robotham and his Clan foundry team began tank engine development it was the Kestrel engine that was initially favoured. The Kestrel, however, gave insufficient power and therefore the Merlin was chosen, minus its supercharging. Leyland Motors, having originally been charged with developing a new engine, built the Meteor-engined Comet tank from 1945, and an example is pictured here while being tested. (Courtesy Bovington Tank Museum)

Right: In addition to Cromwells, Centurions and Comets, Conqueror heavy tanks, as pictured here, were fitted with Meteor engines. The Meteor programme was eventually handed over to the Rover Company in a deal which saw Rolls-Royce take over development of the jet engine. Development of the Merlin saw the engine used for a variety of applications, including marine work when fitted to the Royal Navy's high-speed craft. (Courtesy Bovington Tank Museum)

increase in Rolls-Royce's workforce from 1939 to 1943: from approximately 13,000 employees to 55,600. The Spitfire, with its distinctive engine note, is not the only testimony to Rolls-Royce engineering: the stained glass memorial window to the pilots of the Battle of Britain in the front hall of the Nightingale Road factory is another. The inscription reads 'to the pilots of the Royal Air Force who, in the Battle of Britain, turned the work of our hands into the salvation of our country.'

CHAPTER SEVEN

THE JET AGE

ERNEST HIVES was invited to accept a knighthood for his services to engineering during the early part of World War Two, but he refused on the grounds that he considered it inappropriate to be recognised at a time when forces personnel were making great personal sacrifices. Later during the war, in 1943, he was again invited to accept a title, and once more he refused. He did, nevertheless, agree to being made a Companion of Honour once victory was assured, and was later honoured by being elevated to the peerage. On 16 June 1950 the Honours List announced his Baronetcy. Hives was specific in his choice of title, the Rt Hon. Lord Hives of Duffield, in the County of Derby. Lord Hives made it understood that he accepted the title on behalf of all the people who had helped build Rolls-Royce. By that time the company was the leading force in aero-engine design and manufacturing, and had more experience than any other organisation in building jet engines.

To commemorate the event Lord Hives sent a message to all employees: 'It is my wish that the great honour which has been conferred upon me by His Majesty should be shared by all Rolls-Royce workers.' A special luncheon was arranged in the staff canteen at Nightingale Road and representatives from every department were invited to attend. In his speech Lord Hives referred to the way that working within Rolls-Royce had changed: no more did the R-R board meet in Conduit Street, ending the belief that Nightingale Road Derby, Crewe and Hillington were mere factories distanced from the hub of business in London; no more were company accountants perceived as being a breed apart and above question and criticism. In industrial relations, Rolls-Royce had emerged as the envy of workers everywhere by being among the first companies to acknowledge shop stewards and adopt a full-time convener.

As a man Lord Hives displayed almost unlimited reserves of mental and physical strength – 'Work until it hurts' was his philosophy – and the team around him drove themselves in similar fashion, even to the detriment of their health. In this respect alone Hives shared a similar disposition to Sir Henry Royce. Hives was not a man with whom to trifle, and when there were industrial problems he met them head on. He successfully introduced a number of working practices, even inviting men's wives to the factory to see for themselves the working conditions, and he never let them depart without first

It was through the efforts of Ernest Hives that Rolls-Royce progressed jet engine technology. It was with the Rover Company that Frank (later Sir Frank) Whittle had furthered his invention, and in 1943 development was transferred to Rolls-Royce. Whittle's engine had first been tested with hugely successful results using the Gloster E.28/39 aircraft, and was later subjected to trials when installed in the tail of a Wellington bomber at Rolls-Royce's flight-test establishment at Hucknall, where this photograph was taken. (Courtesy Sir Henry Royce Memorial Foundation)

having tea. This was a popular move and 70 per cent of the male workforce arranged factory visits for their wives. It is not surprising, therefore, that Hives won the respect of even the most ardent trade unionists.

Theories of Jet Propulsion

It was Hives who steered Rolls-Royce into the jet age before the outbreak of World War Two. In June 1939 the company recruited Dr Alan Griffith, who at the time was working for the Royal Aircraft Establishment at Farnborough, and in 1926 had written his outstanding thesis *An Aerodynamic Theory of Turbine Design*. Dr Griffith had then proposed using an axial gas turbine engine to drive a propeller rather than a piston engine, and his theory was proven when, in 1928, experiments were conducted on behalf of the Aeronautical Research Committee. Appointed to the Air Ministry Laboratory in South Kensington during that same year, Griffith developed the principle of contraflow for gas turbine design. His ideas did not materialise until 1939 when Armstrong-Siddeley built an experimental contraflow compressor, by which time Griffith had moved back to Farnborough where he had taken charge of engine design.

The Rolls-Royce Avon engine, elsewhere described as a modern day Merlin, went into production during 1950 specifically for use with the English Electric Canberra bomber, and its concept can be attributed to Dr Griffith. In 1954 he was responsible for the 'flying bedstead', a test rig platform that was launched vertically with the aid of two Rolls-Royce Nene engines, thus pioneering 'vertical take-off and landing' (VTOL).

Jet propulsion had also interested Dr Hans von Ohain who, aged 22 in 1933, conceived the idea of a continuous-cycle combustion engine. Ohain took his ideas to Ernst Heinkel, who offered the young inventor the use of his test facilities. Within three years a complete engine and airframe had been built, and on 27 August 1939 the aircraft took off and completed the world's first jet-powered flight. Surprisingly, the principle of the jet engine was largely

Rolls-Royce's development of the jet engine led to the introduction of the Welland engine, and it was the experience gained from that which led to the Derwent. Design work commenced in April 1943 and first tests were held in July. Designated B.37, the engine developed 2,000lbs thrust and successive variants produced more power, the maximum thrust of the Derwent 8 being 3,600lbs at 14,700rpm. (Courtesy Sir Henry Royce Memorial Foundation)

overlooked by Germany during the early period of the war, nevertheless its presence was felt during the latter years and contributed to Britain's effort in developing the jet engine for military purposes.

Frank Whittle

It was in 1928 that Frank Whittle, who had joined the RAF five years previously as a boy apprentice, published his paper *Future Developments in Aircraft Design* in which he perceived that aeroplanes would not only fly at least twice the speed of the then fastest aircraft, but would also fly at vastly greater altitudes, to take advantage of the rarefied air. It was while he was at Cambridge that Whittle displayed a solid understanding of thermodynamics and supersonic airflow, and his researches took a leap forward in October 1929 when he revealed that the piston engine could be displaced by the gas turbine owing to the exhaust gases propelling an aircraft rather than the propeller.

Following talks with the Air Ministry, arrangements were made for Frank Whittle, by this time a regular RAF officer whose duties included test-piloting a diverse range of aircraft, and Dr Griffith, to meet. The ensuing discussions were not exactly cordial; Griffith was critical of Whittle's calculations and Whittle, having checked his theories, became highly critical of Griffith.

Frank Whittle, having been notified by the Air Ministry that his theory was basically unsound, nevertheless filed a patent for jet propulsion in January 1930, without any support from the aero industry or the Air Ministry. The patent was granted in 1932 and was widely published, but when it came for renewal in 1935 Whittle allowed it to lapse, believing that the resources for successful development of the turbojet engine were unattainable.

Had it not been for a former Cranwell colleague, Whittle's theories of jet propulsion might never have materialised. Rolf Williams, in conjunction with another former RAF pilot, J.C. Tinling, arranged for Whittle to take out further patents and went as far as providing £50,000 to develop a jet-propelled aeroplane. That sum of money was then very substantial, certainly equal to around £2 million 60 years later, and it permitted Whittle to take a leave of absence while he progressed a programme of research. This in turn led to the establishment of Power Jets Limited, and in 1940 the Rover Car Company, through the efforts of Whittle and brothers Maurice and Spencer Wilks, became involved in developing the jet engine. The period between the establishment of Power Jets Limited in 1936 and Rover's involvement was often fraught with despair, and at times it seemed that the entire project was doomed to failure.

Frank Whittle had tried in vain to encourage Armstrong-Siddeley to take an interest in manufacturing an engine, and it was only when British Thomson-Houston became involved (BTH were already committed to working with Rolls-Royce on exhaust-driven superchargers) that the once seemingly impossible appeared potentially promising.

Whittle's engine first ran on 12 April 1937 with almost dire consequences, for when the main valve was opened up and the engine's rpm allowed to accelerate it reached such speed that it threatened to shatter the test house, which was accommodated within an anonymous group of temporary buildings at Lutterworth in Leicestershire. Persevering and paying particular attention to metallurgy and turbine blade design, Whittle ultimately won the approval of the Air Ministry, and it was agreed that the experimental jet engine should be further developed.

The Gloster Trials

The turning point for jet propulsion, as far as Britain was concerned, came in June 1940 when the Ministry of Aircraft Production (MAP), with Lord Beaverbrook at the helm, was formed. Authority was given to progress the development of the Whittle-engined Gloster E.28/39 aircraft, the Air Ministry having placed an order with the Gloster Aircraft Co. for the design and construction of such an aeroplane, and in April the following year it was ready for taxiing trials.

The Gloster underwent trials on 8 April 1941, with test pilot Flight Lieutenant P.E.G. Sayer at the controls. As well as taxiing, Sayer ventured to become airborne over a couple of hundred yards on some three occasions. The reports were encouraging, so much so that the Gloster's official test flight was made a month later on 15 May. That test was a complete success, with Sayer demonstrating every confidence in the aircraft and its engine. A few days later, on 21 May, the Gloster was again in the air to the sheer amazement of a large delegation which included the Secretary of State for Air, Sir Archibald Sinclair, and Geoffrey de Havilland. The Air Ministry responded by immediately setting production targets for 500 aircraft and 1,200 jet engines, the first to be available in June 1942. In the meantime Whittle had much work to do developing the engine, and along with the original W.1 unit there evolved

variants, the W.2 and W.2B. In Whittle's opinion the work did not progress as quickly or smoothly as he would have hoped.

It was, perhaps, only a matter of time before Rolls-Royce became involved with Whittle and the jet engine. Certainly Ernest Hives and his aero-engine designers were very much aware of the development of Whittle's invention, and Hives had first met the inventor while visiting Power Jets in 1940. Hives had originally favoured Griffith's ideas regarding jet propulsion, and it was only later that he changed his opinion to prefer Whittle's approach. The link between Hives and Whittle was Stanley Hooker, who had held discussions with Whittle, and following the visit to Power Jets an offer was quickly made by Rolls-Royce to manufacture turbine blades and other components that were in short supply. Supplying parts to Power Jets evolved into an offer by Rolls-Royce to build for Whittle a version of his engine. That in fact did not happen and Power Jets Limited remained as principal contractor, while Rolls-Royce was nominated sub-contractor.

Behind the scenes at Nightingale Road, Sir Henry Tizard, chairman of the Joint Production and Development Committee at the MAP, had encouraged Hives to facilitate manufacturing certain components that required Rolls-Royce's expertise. Hives was unhappy that Rolls-Royce would become merely a jobbing contractor, or as he put it a little less respectfully, 'a maker of bits'.

In 1941 the MAP's deputy director of scientific research, Dr Roxbee Cox, was visiting Nightingale Road when Hives suggested to him that development of the jet engine was of such importance that it should be treated as a national effort.

It was Hives's opinion that those companies engaged on work involving the jet engine should be brought together under a committee representing all interests. Hives's proposal was adopted, and the subsequent committee became known as the Gas Turbine Collaboration Committee, and was chaired by Dr Cox.

Rolls-Royce and Rover Do a Deal

Having been commissioned to build Whittle's engines, Rover was blamed by Whittle for contributing to delays in production. The evidence is that relations between Whittle and Rover were fragile to say the least, and Maurice Wilks was finding working with the inventor very tedious. That Wilks would have been happy to remove Rover from the Whittle project was apparent – after all, Rover was first and foremost a motor manufacturer – and his chance came when he met Ernest Hives over lunch one day at the Swan and Royal at Clitheroe. Hives was equally anxious to take on Rover's involvement, and came up with a plan that was acceptable to all concerned.

Hives took a direct approach and asked Maurice Wilks what Rover were doing with the jet engine project. Without waiting for an answer, Hives made an offer whereby Rolls-Royce would exchange its Meteor tank engine work for Rover's jet engine business, production of the former being ideally accommodated at Rover's Solihull shadow factory. Thus the deal was done. As for Whittle – by now he was Air Commodore Whittle – he expressed his pleasure at Rolls-Royce's involvement, which both parties agreed was in the interest of the national effort. That lunch, incidentally, was possibly the most profitable for Rolls-Royce. There was a directive within the company that decreed that lunch expenses should amount to no more than five shillings, and that is exactly what the meal cost. That lunch came close to changing history.

With the acquisition of the Whittle jet engine in the spring of 1943 (Rover had started to hand over control at the end of 1942) Rolls-Royce inherited the services of Adrian Lombard, a young Rover engineer with outstanding credentials who stayed with Rolls-Royce throughout his working life. With Rolls-Royce at the helm the pace of jet engine development quickened: Stanley Hooker was put in charge of operations and he was ably assisted by Geoff Wilde, Les Buckler, Fred Morley and Ron Kibby. The MAP favoured the arrangement to the extent that they envisaged that Rolls-Royce would take over Power Jets, but in the event Rolls-Royce considered the firm's valuation to be too high given its assets, and Power Jets had no desire to lose its independence. The fact that development of the jet engine was at last secure in the hands of Rolls-Royce is remarkable given that Ernest Hives had willingly confessed that initially he had been highly sceptical of the engine and its concept.

As might be supposed a great amount of background work was conducted in the lead-up to Hives's offer to Maurice Wilks. Ernest Hives had already established that it was Rolls-Royce that should be undertaking the gas turbine business, not Rover, and Frank Whittle, after a number of encouraging meetings with Hives and Stanley Hooker at Derby, had suggested as much. The company's flight-test establishment at Hucknall had been testing the Whittle engine with excellent results, and Ray Dorey was instrumental in arranging for a Wellington bomber to be made available in order that the engine might be tested in its tail.

As to the production of the Whittle engine, that was initially undertaken at Barnoldswick in Lancashire, although Nightingale Road was greatly involved in the design process. Under the direction of Rolls-Royce the Whittle engine became known as the Welland, the first of a series of engines taking their names from rivers.

At the Gloster Aircraft Company the Meteor was meanwhile being developed as a single-seat twin-jet fighter to Air Ministry specification F.9/40. According to *Jane's All The World's Aircraft* the Gloster Meteor first flew in March 1943. A little over a year later, in May 1944, the RAF took delivery of the first batch of Meteor Is, which were allocated to the Royal Aircraft Establishment at Farnborough and then transferred to Manston in Kent under the command of 616 Squadron. The first duty the Meteors were assigned was the interception of German V1 flying bombs, success being assured when a Meteor shot one down on 14 August. There is evidence that Meteor pilots had the resources to fly alongside the V1s and, using the tips of the jet aircraft's wings, tilted the flying bombs sufficiently that they crashed into the sea.

Apart from it being the world's first production jet-engined aeroplane, the Gloster Meteor proved to be a huge success in its own right. In excess of 3,500 Meteors of different variants were built in the UK and Benelux countries in the decade 1944 to 1954, and they served throughout Europe as well as in Britain.

The Welland and the Derwent

The Welland engine passed its 100-hour type-test in April 1943. Having a reverse-flow combustion system it developed 1,700lbs thrust, although initial engines were derated to 1,450lbs. Ronald Harker, recalling the period when the Meteor was being tested at Hucknall, refers to piloting those early jets as being an interesting experience, as they had slow acceleration owing to the engine's low thrust threshold. Once in the air the Meteor proved to be highly manoeuvrable and totally outpaced piston-engined fighters. Harker relates how the Gloster jets were kept so secret that not even the average squadron pilot knew of their existence, and were astounded at the speed the aircraft approached them in the air, and equally astonished at the speed at which they flew away compared to conventional machines.

Rolls-Royce was not the only British aero-engine manufacturer to be developing the gas-turbine engine. In this respect Ernest Hives appreciated that the company had to have an established lead. Other manufacturers concerned with jet engines were Armstrong-Siddeley with its ASX and ASP units, Bristol with the Theseus, De Havilland with the H-1 Goblin and Metropolitan-Vickers with the F.2/4. Elsewhere jet engines were being developed in Germany by BMW, Daimler-Benz, Heinkel-Hirth and Junkers, and in America by General Motors and Westinghouse.

The Derwent engine (otherwise known as the B37) was a more powerful version of the Welland and was being developed alongside it. Having straight-through combustion the Derwent provided 2,000lbs thrust and was designed to fit into the standard Meteor nacelle. It could therefore be regarded as a replacement or alternative to the Welland. Ready for testing in July 1943, the drawings for the Derwent had been started only three months earlier; in November the 100-hour type-test was completed and the engine was put into production in April 1944. Development of the Derwent programme produced the Derwent II and IV with 2,200lbs and 2,400lbs thrust respectively. There was also a Derwent III which was used for special purposes and remained an experimental engine.

When the Derwent V was introduced it demonstrated twice the thrust of the

Derwent I, and it is this engine which powered the Meteor to establish a world speed record averaging 606mph. The record was attained on 7 November 1945, when a Gloster Meteor IV piloted by Group Captain H.J. Wilson made four runs over a 3km speed course off Herne Bay in Kent. On the same day an identical aeroplane flown by Gloster's chief test pilot, Eric Greenwood, averaged 603mph over the same course.

The Derwent programme was largely initiated by Air Commodore Rod Banks, who was director of engine research at the Air Ministry. Banks had communicated with Ernest Hives, who was only too aware of the Welland's shortcomings: it did not offer the power potential that was required to make the Gloster fighter fully effective. Both Hives and Banks feared that if the Welland was not developed to produce substantially more power, there remained the possibility that the Air Ministry might view the entire project as ineffective and allow other countries to take Britain's lead. Banks agreed that the jet engine offered the key to future aero-engine development, but was sceptical about whether it would have any real influence during the remainder of World War Two.

The jet engine therefore had to demonstrate substantial benefits over the piston-type aero-engines that were then available, as well as those that were under development. The criterion, according to Air Commodore Banks, was to achieve 2,000lbs thrust as a minimum, which is exactly what was achieved with the Derwent I. In the longer term Hives perceived that jet engines had a far-reaching role post-war, something that appeared not to be fully appreciated at the Air Ministry.

Hives did have some allies at the MAP, among whom were Rod Banks and the chief executive Sir Wilfred Freeman. Both were anxious that the jet engine be developed in a military capacity as well as for civilian use, and therefore in 1944 the MAP authorised Rolls-Royce to build the Nene engine. The specification was that the turbojet engine should provide a minimum static thrust of 4,000lbs, have a weight of no more than 2,200lbs and a maximum diameter of 55 inches. Early considerations had looked at scaling up the Derwent engine to meet the specification, but doing so would have meant that the diameter would have had to be increased to almost 60 inches. A completely new engine development was put in hand and, remarkably, was completed in a little over five months. Although it can be claimed that the Nene was a descendant of the Derwent, it nevertheless can be acknowledged as the first jet engine to have been designed and developed entirely by Rolls-Royce.

The Nene

For Rolls-Royce and military aviation world wide, the jet age had truly arrived. Jet-powered fighters had the capacity to out manoeuvre piston-engined aircraft under virtually all circumstances. Acknowledging that by the end of the war the RAF would be left with fleets of outdated aeroplanes, Hives told Sir Wilfred Freeman as much. Just as Freeman had been instrumental in re-equipping the RAF in times of hostilities, Hives told him he should adopt the same principle in peacetime.

As if to exemplify the very situation that Hives had perceived, when it came to test-flying the Nene engine there was no suitable British military aeroplane to fit it to. According to Ronald Harker, early trials had been conducted using a Lancaster bomber converted to civilian use, thus becoming the Lancastrian, whereby the two outboard Merlins had been supplanted with Nenes. To test-fly the Nene under conditions that had originally been envisaged, a Lockheed P80 Shooting Star was acquired.

The Nene engine proved to be highly successful and was used in the Hawker Sea Hawk and Supermarine's Attacker, along with a variety of American machines including the Shooting Star. The Nene gave way to the Tay, which, like its predecessor, was used in a number of military applications, although few of them were in the United Kingdom. The Tay did emerge in America, where it was built as the Pratt & Whitney J48, and in France under the direction of Hispano-Suiza.

During the latter years of World War Two Rolls-Royce shared its gas-turbine technology not only with some of its European neighbours but also with America and the Soviet Union. The lead that Rolls-Royce, and the Derby factory in particular, had gained was therefore largely diluted in the immediate post-war period, and it can be claimed that as a result of wartime politics both the British government, the nation, and Rolls-Royce forfeited substantial earnings in later years. Regarding the sale of Derwent and Nene engines to the Soviet Union, which had been instigated by the Labour government under the support of Sir Stafford Cripps, Minister of Economic Affairs, Rolls-Royce refused to allow Soviet representatives in any of its factories, nor would it divulge any specifications for the complex materials that were used in the manufacture of some of the engine's components, including the turbine blades. In doing this Rolls-Royce believed that the Soviets would be unable to duplicate the parts, especially as they did not have a manufacturing license, but in the event the company discovered that the engines had indeed been reproduced, in a surprisingly short time, and they appeared on the Mig-15s and Mig-17s, both types of aircraft which were used in the Korean war in combat against America.

The fact that the jet engine saw combat service with the Gloster Meteor and the DH Vampire to what was then seen as the ultimate effect, allowed the British government, to its cost, to relax its stance on military aviation development. Nevertheless Rolls-Royce, and Ernest Hives in particular, maintained that the jet engine had such a powerful force in world aviation that after the war the Nightingale Road factory would continue to serve the aviation industry. The resumption of motor car production, viewed by Hives as being essential to Rolls-Royce's core business, would have to be undertaken elsewhere.

There were two choices of location for production of motor cars: Hillington and Crewe. Hillington might have been the obvious choice, for the Glasgow factory had a suitable foundry and certainly the premises were sufficiently large to support car making. What let it down in Hives's opinion was its location, together with its industrial relations record. The choice was therefore Crewe, with its pool of highly skilled technicians. The decision to make Crewe the car manufacturing base was taken as early as 1943, and once the war was at an end work began transferring from aero-engine production. The Clan foundry, the wartime base of the chassis division, was eventually moved to Crewe, but not before the factory was producing motor cars and Roy Robotham's proposals for rationalisation had been put firmly put into action. Of the cars that were produced at Crewe there is requirement for only the briefest of detail, for the Crewe story has been told elsewhere.

Emphasis was placed on the Bentley marque initially, the Mark VI being the first car to leave the production lines. For the first time in its history a Rolls-Royce motor car was built as a complete product, coachwork to a standard design being supplied by Pressed Steel, providers of vehicle bodies to a good percentage of Britain's car makers including Rover. The Rolls-Royce Silver Wraith made its debut shortly afterwards and in Rolls-Royce tradition was supplied as a chassis only. Customers could then specify coachwork from a preferred coachbuilder. The post-war bespoke coachbuilding industry was in a lesser position that it had been at the end of the 1930s, many firms having not survived the war years. Customers could also select the Bentley as a chassis only in order that bespoke coachwork be supplied. It was only later that the Silver Dawn was introduced; available initially for export orders, it could be supplied with either the standard bodyshell or as a chassis. The reason for promoting the Bentley marque was largely political, as in the period of post-war austerity it was seen as being less ostentatious than Rolls-Royce. Needless to say there was no difference in quality between the two cars.

In transferring motor car production to Crewe there was some relocating of key personnel. Roy Robotham was appointed chief engineer of the chassis division, while the general manager was Dr Frederick Llewellyn Smith, who had joined Rolls-Royce at Nightingale Road in 1933 as a technical assistant working on aero-engines. During the war Llewellyn Smith was appointed to Hillington, and when hostilities were at an end he had the unenviable task of running the workforce down from 26,000 to 15,000. Working under Ivan Evernden was John Blatchley who, having joined Rolls-Royce at Hucknall in the late 1930s, where he had designed aero-engine cowlings, was later to be appointed chief stylist.

Sir Stanley Hooker Resigns

There was much reorganisation within the aero division of Rolls-Royce. At Nightingale Road there were also huge reductions in the number of personnel, and overall some 25,000 workforce positions were lost. Gas-turbine research and design was based at Derby with Adrian Lombard becoming chief designer in 1946, a move which caused certain difficulties for Hives, when Sir Stanley Hooker tendered his resignation and went to Bristol Siddeley Engines. While Sir Stanley Hooker's departure from Rolls-Royce could well have given Hives grounds for animosity towards both him and his new employer, it failed to do so. In fact when Bristol was experiencing serious technical problems with its Proteus engine, it was Hives who offered to provide assistance, and within hours some of Nightingale Road's most experienced engineers were despatched to Bristol Siddeley.

It was not only gas-turbine engines for jet propulsion that Rolls-Royce was concerned with during the early post-war era. Further development of the piston engine ceased when Merlin and Griffon production halted, but there remained a market for a new generation of propeller engines driven by gas

It was during the mid-1940s that Rolls-Royce developed the Trent turboprop engine, the first of its type in Britain. Built for experimental purposes only, it did, however, lead to the development of the Dart engine, a compact turboprop which was fitted to the Viscount airliner. The engine featured a two-stage centrifugal compressor that afforded approximately 20lbs of air per second, and a two-stage turbine. For some years the Viscount was the mainstay of several airlines, including BEA. (Courtesy Sir Henry Royce Memorial Foundation)

turbine. These attracted the name turbo-prop. As for the jet airliner of the future, there was some dilemma, for there was no real indication as to what form it would take.

Rolls-Royce's first turbo-prop engine was the Trent, which was built purely for experimental purposes. It was also the first turbo-prop to take to the air when, following testing in March 1945, two units were installed in a Meteor fighter. The company's first commercial turbo-prop was the Dart, which saw service with the Vickers Viscount airliner, a world favourite and one that was extensively used by British European Airways among other United Kingdom and European operators. In addition to the Viscount the Dart was used in the Fokker Friendship, Handley Page Herald and the BAe 748 series of aircraft. A larger and more powerful turbo-prop was the Tyne which, in addition to being specified for the Vickers Vanguard airliner, was fitted to the Fairey Rotodyne multi-engined helicopter. The concept of the latter was an inter-city commuter aircraft which failed to materialise for a number of reasons, one being that it suffered from questionable performance.

The Brabazon Committee

During the aftermath of war it was left to the Brabazon Committee to decide the future direction of Britain's civil aviation industry. The Transport Aircraft Committee, which was made up largely of civil servants, had first met in 1942 and it was that meeting which had led to the establishment the following year of a body incorporating mostly aviation executives under the chairmanship of Lord Brabazon. It was this committee that envisaged specific aircraft types encompassing all market sectors. While the committee planned and calculated much of the emphasis was lost to the Americans. For Rolls-Royce the situation might have been catastrophic, in that sales of aero-engines had been largely to British manufacturers. Rolls-Royce nevertheless had a fine reputation in America where the company's cars were revered. The fact that the Merlin engine, built in the US by Packard, was widely appreciated helped boost Rolls-Royce's standing. Therefore when Hives and his select team of sales engineers travelled the world marketing Rolls-Royce engines they were often warmly received by airframe manufacturers.

What did emerge was the Rolls-Royce Avon-powered de Havilland Comet airliner, the world's first jet airliner. Originally conceived as the AJ65, because of its 6,500lb thrust, development began in 1945 at Barnoldswick under the direction of Stanley Hooker. There were delays and problems with the testing of the engine and ultimately Hives decided that development should be transferred to Nightingale Road. Making its debut in 1948, the Avon was test flown in an Avro Lancastrian with Rolls-Royce's chief test pilot R.T. Shepherd at the controls. The Avon was fitted to the English Electric Canberra bomber in 1949, and to a twin-engined Gloster Meteor, allowing that aircraft's performance to be pushed beyond all expected limits.

What makes the Avon particularly significant in Rolls-Royce aero-engine history is that it heralded a departure from centrifugal flow and a move to axial flow. Thus it was possible to achieve considerably improved thrust ratings, as well as all-important fuel efficiencies. The comparison with the Merlin engine has nothing to do with design of course, but because the Avon has been produced in vast numbers.

It was the Korean war of 1950 that boosted sales of the Avon, and in addition to the Canberra the engine was applied to the Vickers Valiant bomber along with the Hawker Hunter and Swift fighters. It was not only at Nightingale Road that the Avon was put into production. Because of the surge in orders for military purposes Hillington was tooled for the Avon, and licenses for production were awarded to Napier and Bristol as well as the Standard Motor Company. Avons were built overseas too, in Australia and Sweden.

The Comet

Comet development was begun in 1943 by de Havilland and the company originally specified their own Ghost engine. Ultimately the more powerful Avon became the preferred choice, and Avon-powered Comets were, by 1953, making regular test flights with outstanding results. When the Comet 1 went into service it was, however, powered by the Ghost engines, which limited the aircraft's capacity to 36 passengers and a range of 2,000 miles at no more than 460mph. BOAC were one of the airlines operating Comet 1s, but others waited for the more powerful Avon-powered Comet 2. The euphoria derived from those initial trials and operating successes dramatically and tragically ended when two aircraft crashed for no obvious reason.

The Comet was the world's first jet-powered airliner and was being developed by de Havilland as early as 1944. The aircraft was first flown in 1949 and the first scheduled passenger service commenced in May 1952 on the Johannesburg route. Early Comets suffered from some mysterious fatal accidents, the cause being traced to metal fatigue. Mk 2 Comets were fitted with Rolls-Royce Avon 503 engines, and the Mk 4 and its derivatives were used for some years on transatlantic services. This emotive photograph neatly defines the supersonic age with the Avon-powered Comet and another prestigious Rolls-Royce product, the Bentley R-Type Continental. When introduced in 1952, the Bentley Continental was the fastest and most expensive production saloon car in Britain. (Courtesy Rolls-Royce & Bentley Motor Cars Ltd)

The problem with the Comet eventually emerged as being a weakness in the cabin structure. It had taken de Havilland and the Royal Aircraft Establishment an enormous amount of time to establish the difficulty and for de Havilland's engineers to redesign the aircraft which, four years after the crashes, evolved as the Comet 4. With its Avon engines Comet 4s provided unequalled service and many remained in operation around the world for many years. Not least, the Comet 4 progressed into the Nimrod reconnaissance aircraft, which remain in service, powered by the Rolls-Royce Spey engine.

Avon engines were used in a number of other aeroplanes, including the supersonic Lightning fighter, and the French Caravelle airliner, which was the first to adopt a tail-mounted configuration. On 10 March 1956 a Fairey Delta Two aircraft piloted by Peter Twiss was the first to achieve a speed in excess of 1,000mph to establish a record of 1,132mph.

The lead in civil aviation that the Comet airliner had established was lost in the intervening period between the fateful crashes and the introduction of the Comet 4. From America a new generation of aircraft had materialised in the shape of the Pratt & Whitney-powered Boeing 707 and Douglas DC-8, both highly successful designs which enjoyed long careers.

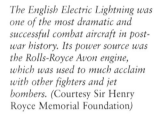

CHAPTER EIGHT

MODERN TIMES

T HE DEMAND for aero-engines in the wake of the onset of the Korean War placed unprecedented pressures on the Derby factory. The fact that Avon engines had been manufactured away from Rolls-Royce had been the outcome of Lord Hives's efforts to relieve some of that pressure; had he not taken such action Rolls-Royce would have undergone a rapid programme of expansion which would have resulted, later, in serious over-capacity.

During the 1950s the Derby works did expand. World War Two had highlighted the need for diesel engines for use in commercial vehicles, and it was appreciated that aero-engine practice had a particular role to play keeping weights to a minimum. There might have been a proposal to establish Rolls-Royce's diesel engine manufacturing at Crewe along with car assembly, but in the event Lord Hives took the decision to base the oil-engine division at Derby and appointed Roy Robotham as director and general manger. The Sinfin B site was chosen to accommodate the works, which were built complete with their own office block in Victory Road, Derby.

One of the reasons for not establishing the oil-engine division at Crewe was political, as beneath Rolls-Royce's calm outward appearance there was some turmoil between senior personalities. The fact that Dr Llewellyn Smith had been brought in from the aero division to operate the chassis division was unpalatable to the more senior Robotham, and there is an indication that he considered resigning from the company over the appointment. Robotham nevertheless had certain qualities that Hives could not afford to lose, and by moving him to Derby in a newly created position Hives resolved a number of issues. The oil-engine factory had originally been constructed to build engines for the Vickers crawler tractor, which had been designed to compete with the 200hp Caterpillar product.

The American Caterpillar bulldozer was, at the time, a world-leading product. Although reliable, it was nevertheless basic and lacking in sophistication. Vickers, on the other hand, thought their bulldozer more powerful and with better all-round performance; not only was it designed to provide more efficient control, it was intended to offer the operator more refined comfort. Having the Rolls-Royce engine, Vickers was able to claim that its machine was 4mph faster than Caterpillar's, that it was easier to start and that it gave unmatched levels of torque. There was no doubt that the Vickers

For Rolls-Royce the Conway engine was a completely new venture, for this was a new type of jet which pioneered 'bypass' technology. Lower exhaust velocity and quieter operation were features of the engine, which was applied to a range of aircraft including the Handley Page Victor bomber. (Courtesy Sir Henry Royce Memorial Foundation)

machine met all its maker's promises, but there were, nonetheless, a number of problems that ultimately led to its downfall. The Caterpillar's suspension proved to be more durable than that the Vickers, and customers discovered to their cost that service and maintenance created downtimes that were too excessive. When Vickers introduced a modified tractor, that, too, failed to attractive sufficient customers. The outcome was that Vickers scrapped the entire project after having built 1,200 vehicles, thus leaving Rolls-Royce with an inordinate amount of capacity. Despite there being other projects which were profitable, the oil-engine division was forced to seek alternative contracts, and its eventual success culminated in the acquisition of the Shrewsbury-based Sentinel company in 1957. With Sentinel's acquisition it was decided to move the oil division away from Derby and establish both operations at Shrewsbury.

Lord Hives Retires

It was in 1957 that Lord Hives retired from Rolls-Royce. Talking to, and listening to those who knew him, it is apparent that Hives's tenure at Rolls-Royce guaranteed the company's success after Sir Henry Royce's death. Hives was first and foremost a brilliant engineer, and as a gifted manager of personnel there was no equal; of quiet disposition he was nevertheless assertive, and as a measure of the man, when he was made a peer he was provided with a Phantom IV, the model of Rolls-Royce that was strictly reserved for royalty and heads of state. Hives seldom used the Phantom, preferring instead the Bentley R-Type, his favourite car, and the Phantom IV was eventually disposed of.

That Lord Hives had guided Rolls-Royce through some very difficult times is not in doubt. When he was appointed general manager Rolls-Royce was, in relation to some aero-engine companies, hardly a volume producer, but in two decades that was reversed, and the company was recognised as being at the leading edge of technology.

Succeeding Hives was Denning (later Sir Denning) Pearson, who had joined Rolls-Royce in 1932 and was appointed to the Nightingale Road design office. His career took an upward turn when the Hillington factory opened, and it was there that Denning Pearson became head of the technical department, a precursor to being appointed chief technical production engineer. When Rolls-Royce established a technical office in Montreal it was Pearson who was destined to head it, for he had had much to do with the Packard Merlin engines that were used to power aircraft ordered by Trans Canada Airlines and the Royal Canadian Air Force. Furthermore he had been instrumental in advising Hives that the company should be a major player in commercial aviation once World War Two was at an end.

Denning Pearson was appointed general manager, aero-engines sales and service in 1949, and at the same time was offered a place on the Rolls-Royce board. That appointment led to him being appointed managing director of the aero-engine division in 1954, and in 1957 he took on the additional responsibility of being chief executive and deputy chairman under Lord Kindersley on Lord Hives's retirement.

Mergers and Rationalisation

The late 1950s were a period of much change in the aviation industry, and similar to events that were then taking place in the British motor industry, there were mergers and acquisitions to the extent that some famous names disappeared. Hawker Siddeley Aviation (HSA) was created in 1960 by amalgamating the Hawker Siddeley Group, which had been formed in 1935, with Folland Aircraft, Blackburn and de Havilland. At the same time, Vickers-Armstrong, English Electric, Hunting and Bristol Aircraft combined to form the British Aircraft Corporation (BAC).

Elsewhere in the industry the interests of Westland Aircraft, Saunders-Roe and the helicopter element of Fairey Aviation, together with that of Bristol Aircraft, were amassed as Westland Helicopters, while Westland Aircraft were instrumental in establishing the British Hovercraft Corporation when Saunders-Roe hovercraft interests were acquired.

With the British aviation industry set in a new direction there remained optimism that an exciting and lucrative future lay ahead. The changes that took place had consequences for the British aero-engine business, and, similar to the plight of airframe manufacturers, a series of take-overs and mergers altered the entire structure of the industry. In 1958 Bristol Aero-engines and Armstrong-Siddeley Motors merged to form Bristol Siddeley Engines, and in 1961 BSE bought Blackburn Engines and the de Havilland Engine Company from the Hawker Siddeley Group.

During the early 1960s there were, therefore, two major aero-engine manufacturers in Britain, Bristol Siddeley and Rolls-Royce. The mergers brought about a level of confidence which was heightened by statements made by Edward Bowyer, who was then chairman of the Society of British Aerospace Companies, predicting that the government and industry were set to establish closer cooperation. That euphoria, sadly, was not destined to last. A series of damaging events during the first half of the 1960s led not only to a loss of confidence in the British aero industry, but also serious consequences for Rolls-

Royce. Those events eventually materialised in the acquisition, in 1966, of Bristol Siddeley by Rolls-Royce.

With Bristol Siddeley incorporated within Rolls-Royce, Sir Stanley Hooker was reunited with Derby. With Lord Hives in retirement the company was run along very different lines and any hard feelings that might have existed were forgotten.

Rolls-Royce had been greatly involved in the Blue Streak project of the

Conway engines were used for the VC10 long-distance airliner, one of the most successful commercial airliners. In these two photographs Rolls-Royce aero-engine technology combines with the prestige that is associated with Rolls-Royce motor cars. Both Derby and Crewe are represented here, the former with aero-engines and the latter with the Rolls-Royce Silver Cloud. Much under-rated, the VC10 was used by the RAF from 1967 for VIP and troop transport, and from 1987 as in-flight tankers, a role they still fulfil. (Courtesy Sir Henry Royce Memorial Foundation)

1950s, which had relied upon the company's RZ-2 motors. When the weapons system was cancelled it was not only Rolls-Royce that suffered; as a consequence of the government's decision to pull out of the development, it was the many associated contractors and sub-contractors that were harmed. The Tyne-engined Fairey Rotodyne vertical take-off airliner project was another setback for Rolls-Royce when government support was withdrawn in 1962. Following the general election in 1964, when a Labour government came to power, there was a period of much uncertainty while industry and commerce waited to see how the defence programme was going to differ from that of the outgoing Conservative government. Within months the TSR2 programme, along with Hawker-Siddeley's P-1154 VTO fighter undertaking, was scrapped, which left Bristol Siddeley, who were supplying the engines, in an invidious position. Rolls-Royce was at the time developing the Medway engine for the Hawker-Siddeley short take-off and landing aircraft, the HS-681, which was also cancelled.

The situation could have been worse for Rolls-Royce had the company not forged relations with the American and French aero industries. Work continued with Turbomeca of France in developing and building the Adour engine specified for the Jaguar strike aircraft among others, and in America cooperation persisted with Allison on the TF-41, a military version of the Rolls-Royce Spey engine.

In addition to military aircraft, in this instance the Phantom fighter, the Spey engine was fitted to Trident and One-Eleven airliners. This photograph shows the re-enactment by a Phantom of the pioneering flight by Alcock and Brown across the Atlantic in 1919. The Phantom is piloted by Sqn Ldr Tony Alcock MBE and Flt Lt W.M. Browne. (Courtesy Sir Henry Royce Memorial Foundation)

A New Era: The Long-Range Civil Airliner

The age of the long-range civil airliner had arrived with the introduction of the Boeing 707 and Douglas DC8. Long-distance flights became a reality and it was at last possible to fly non-stop on transatlantic routes. There was no question of Rolls-Royce not being committed to compete against American aero-engine makers Pratt & Whitney, which had initially dominated the market sector. Rolls-Royce therefore introduced the Conway engine, which was largely designed and inspired by Adrian Lombard.

The Conway was significantly dissimilar to the Pratt & Whitney engine, and heralded the 'by-pass' type of engine. It was with the Conway that Rolls-Royce pioneered 'by-pass' technology, whereby some of the intake air was ducted to the hotter parts of the engine so that it was heated through heat transfer before being fed into the exhaust gases. By-pass engines were demonstrated to achieve a lower exhaust velocity in addition to being both fuel efficient and quieter in operation.

When both BOAC and TCA placed orders for the Boeing 707 it was presumed there would be no question of either airline not specifying the Conway engine. TCA did in fact opt for the Conway, but BOAC made no decision apart from allowing the airframe manufacturer to fit the most appropriate unit. Boeing chose the Conway, although BOAC had been inclined towards the Pratt & Whitney. The first Rolls-Royce powered 707s entered service in 1960, and thereafter a number of operators followed TCA's and BOAC's lead, although the great majority showed preference for the American engine.

The successor to the Conway was the RB211, which Rolls-Royce began developing in the early 1960s in order to compete with the 'big thrust' engines then being proposed by the American aviation industry. A new generation of airliners, the wide-bodied jets, were being developed, and to remain at the forefront of the aero-engine market Rolls-Royce had to be able to offer an alternative to those engines being proposed by General Electric and Pratt & Whitney. The sheer enormity of the RB211 is evident in this photograph, which shows an engine on test. A feature of the RB211 was its technically advanced Hyfil fan blades, which were initially highly successful but were ultimately proved to be flawed because they did not pass the all-essential 'bird strike' tests. (Courtesy Sir Henry Royce Memorial Foundation)

Before being made available for civil use, Conway engines served successfully in a number of military applications. Most significant was the Handley Page Victor bomber and aerial tanker.

The BAC VC10 and Super VC10, which were built for BOAC's long haul services to Africa and the Far East were specified to use Conway engines. These elegant aircraft, with their four-engine arrangement mounted at the tail, had an enviable service record and for a number of years were used by the RAF.

During the late 1950s British European Airways issued specifications for a jet-powered rather than a turbo-prop airliner for its medium and short-haul services. Rolls-Royce Spey engines were specified for this three-engined aeroplane that entered service as the Trident with its power units fitted at the rear of the fuselage. Later Tridents had stretched fuselages and were fitted with an additional boost engine, RB162, positioned in the tail to improve take off. Speys were also fitted to another of the British aviation industry's most successful aeroplanes, the BAC One-Eleven.

The Spey was also the first choice of Boeing when that company was developing the 727 airliner. As it happened the Pratt & Whitney JT-8D was ultimately selected, but the Spey was specified for several military aircraft, among which were the Buccaneer and the McDonnell F4 Phantom. In conjunction with Allison the Spey was also specified for the USAAF Corsair.

Triumph and Tragedy: The RB211

Although British aero-engine manufacturers failed to fully break into the American market of aeroplanes that were the Boeing 707, 727 and Douglas DC8, Rolls-Royce in particular set its sights on a wholly new development in world aviation, the wide-bodied jet. A new age was dawning, during which long-haul services would be flown by aircraft such as Lockheed's Tristar, the Douglas DC10 and Boeing's 747 Jumbo Jet. From the outset Rolls-Royce planned to compete head-on with its rival American manufacturers, and therefore work began in the early 1960s developing the RB211.

Had Rolls-Royce not decided to develop the RB211, the potential lead in providing British engines for the new generation of aircraft would have been lost. For Rolls-Royce the situation would have been even more dire because as an engine-maker the company would have risked losing much of its standing.

The 1960s was therefore a period in Rolls-Royce's history that was both influential and vitally important to the company's long-term future, in addition to the potentially substantial foreign currency earnings. The acquisition of Bristol Siddeley meant that Rolls-Royce took on board a number of significant projects, not least the development of Olympus engines, one version, the 593, being intended for the Concorde supersonic airliner, another for the Vulcan bomber. Before the merger Bristol Siddeley had been in joint development with SNECMA of France regarding the Olympus engine, with the result that Rolls-Royce, too, became subsequently involved. The combined operations of Rolls-Royce and Bristol Siddeley resulted in there being a complexity of factories, that at Filton specialising in Olympus research and development, which added up to a workforce in excess of 80,000. As for Concorde, the supersonic airliner has acquired an excellent safety record despite the tragic accident near Paris in

2000. It was not only aircraft that the Olympus was destined to power; the aircraft carrier HMS *Invincible* was fitted with the same engines.

The RB211 programme of development began at a time when America's aero-engine builders had already started to explore comparative engines which had mainly been envisaged to power the C-5A Galaxy freighter. That development would carry over to the wide-bodied jets that were then being planned. As far as Rolls-Royce was concerned, to make the RB211 viable the company would have to win a contract supplying at least one major airframe manufacturer.

The market for wide-bodied jets was effectively opened when Pan-American ordered a fleet of Boeing 747s fitted with Pratt & Whitney JT9D engines. There was obvious disappointment at Derby when it was known that Rolls-Royce had been beaten in the race to supply engines for the new generation aircraft; there was, nevertheless, optimism that Rolls-Royce might be favoured by either Douglas or Lockheed, or both.

The impetus to develop the RB211 initially came from Lockheed, that company having been invited by American Airlines to build a high-capacity jet capable of long distances that could take off and land on relatively short runways. A two-engined airliner had been envisaged, but it was apparent that a three-engined machine would have greater appeal to other airlines. Rolls-Royce responded to Lockheed by offering the RB211-06, an engine with a number of innovative features that had required a huge amount of development.

The offer to supply the RB211 was made on 23 June 1967, with a view to putting the engine into service in 1971. Thereafter the effort to win the Lockheed order was sufficiently substantial to warrant Sir David Huddie, then managing director of the aero-engine division, taking his top executives to America, where they were to reside throughout the lengthy period of negotiations. The competition to win the order was fierce, and to achieve their objective meant the most sustained sales campaign in Rolls-Royce's history to that date. When it was announced on 29 March 1968 that the order had been won there was jubilation throughout British industry, and not least at Derby where the entire city celebrated. Winning the Lockheed order meant supplying engines for 94 Lockheed L-1011 airliners, which became known as TriStars.

The costs involved in developing the RB211 were estimated to be £91.4 million, the largest civil capital investment the company had undertaken. It was not an investment that Rolls-Royce could sustain unaided, and approaches were made to the government of the day for financial assistance. Exactly three months after having won the Lockheed order the British government announced that aid of up to 70 per cent, up to £47.13 million, was being provided to Rolls-Royce. Repayment of the loan was to be effected through levies on engines sales.

In addition to it being Rolls-Royce's greatest financial project, the RB211 constituted the most complex engineering undertaking in the company's history. Not only was the engine physically larger than any previous types, it called for entirely new and different methods of construction. The fact that the engine's fan measured 86 inches in diameter gives some clue about the sheer enormity of the build process, which called for innovative techniques in respect of metal cutting and welding.

The tradition of constructing aero-engines in the horizontal position was lost when Rolls-Royce developed the RB211, which was vertically built. Shown here is the RB211-524 which was fitted to many Boeing 747 jumbo jets. The big thrust engines were originally conceived to power what emerged as the C-5A Galaxy strategic freighter, and the RB211 was initially designed for Lockheed's TriStar airliner. Flight testing the RB211 was conducted using the VC10 airliner, a single engine replacing two Conways. (Courtesy Sir Henry Royce Memorial Foundation)

Arguably the most successful and certainly the best-known airliner of modern times is Concorde. The aircraft's safety record is excellent despite being sadly marred by a fatal accident near Paris. As the aircraft took off, one of its fuel tanks was punctured by debris that had been left on the runway. Powered by four Rolls-Royce Olympus 593 engines, this British Airways Concorde is pictured approaching St Michael's Mount off the Cornish coast. (Courtesy Sir Henry Royce Memorial Foundation)

Development of the RB211 was to cause Rolls-Royce many problems, not least the use of a composite material known as 'Hyfil' for the fan blade construction. Lighter than aluminium but stronger than steel, Hyfil was a carbon fibre that had been jointly developed by Rolls-Royce and the Royal Aircraft Establishment at Farnborough. Another particular difficulty was the continuing requirement for more engine power, which rose from the original 33,250lbs to 42,000lbs. The stresses affecting Rolls-Royce designers during the early development period were enormous, and Adrian Lombard who, as director of engineering, had been responsible for many of the engine's design parameters, succumbed to the strain and died at his desk on 13 July 1967 at the age of 52.

Lombard's premature death was a shock to the Derby development team, and he was greatly missed both as a person and for his engineering expertise. Numerous problems were addressed and the engine was nearing a stage where it could be tested. The RB211 first ran at the end of August 1968, by which time Hyfil blades were being tested in Conway engines fitted to VC10 aircraft. In fact a VC10 was used throughout the testing period when a single RB211 was fitted in place of the left-hand twin Conways to power the aircraft. During the engine's development Lockheed engineers took the unusual step of frequently visiting Nightingale Road to keep abreast of progress. Recalling events at Derby, Ronald Harker makes the point in his autobiography *The Engines Were Rolls-Royce* that Lockheed was financially dependent on Rolls-Royce delivering engines on time and up to specification.

Rolls-Royce officials had worked hard to assure Lockheed that they could deliver on time despite considerable doubts, and there was a general view within the American aviation industry that Rolls-Royce's resources were strained by having too much work.

Major problems beset Rolls-Royce engineers when the RB211 was subjected to the customary 'bird ingestion tests'. The test involves simulating the projection of a four-pound bird at 400mph into an engine's intake without there being any damage to the fan and compressor blades. There is every reason to believe that Nightingale Road engineers did not anticipate any difficulties in this respect, especially as the Hyfil blades had proved so effective during previous testing. When the Hyfil blades shattered on impact with the bird there was despair and disbelief, and the future of Rolls-Royce was immediately in a position of some jeopardy.

The fact that the bird ingestion tests had failed was disastrous in itself, but the situation was compounded by the fact that the project timescale was over-running and costs were spiralling. Exacerbating the position, the fan blades would have to be redesigned using titanium, which meant further delays and a serious escalation of costs.

The effects of the RB211 failure were felt at every level at Nightingale Road. A severe cost-cutting exercise was implemented and at once anything that was considered unnecessary was either curtailed or cancelled. Even porcelain teacups were dispensed with in favour of paper cups. At director level the company Bentleys were called in and sold, and those personnel who were in need of company transport were issued with vehicles of a lesser type.

The Financial Collapse of Rolls-Royce

In the autumn of 1970 the Rolls-Royce board reported to the Ministry of Aviation that the company had run into severe financial difficulties, and that without a further injection of cash amounting to £40 million over two years, it would be unable to continue in business. The government, showing concern over the arrangement to finance the RB211 programme, employed independent accountants to check Rolls-Royce's accounts, the result of which led to some unpalatable decisions, not least terminating cash injections to the company.

Sir Denning Pearson resigned as chairman of Rolls-Royce and was replaced by Lord Cole, who was nominated by the government to lead the company. There was little doubt that the RB211 engine was an excellent design, and that it would be perfected. Such optimism led no one to believe that Rolls-Royce could actually collapse, and indeed Sir Denning Pearson steadfastly maintained that Rolls-Royce's problems were related to financial issues rather than being of a technical nature. Nevertheless, on 22 January 1971 Lord Cole went to the Ministry of Aviation to report that in his view Rolls-Royce was in a desperately serious position. The government was advised that should it bolster Rolls-Royce financially it would run the risk of being legally liable for the company's debts, which meant that the board had to halt the RB211 programme.

On 3 February 1971 the government accepted that there was no alternative other than for Rolls-Royce to appoint a receiver. The following day the Rolls-Royce board met at 8.45am to agree a statement to the effect that it had appointed E. Rupert Nicholson of Peat Marwick Mitchell & Co. as receiver, and that all trading in Rolls-Royce shares was suspended on the London Stock Exchange. The previous day's events, along with that morning's devastating news, was broadcast over the factory's tannoy system. The atmosphere at Nightingale Road was one of shock, and there are reports of employees standing to attention, rigid with disbelief in the knowledge that the very heart of British industry had been struck down. News of Rolls-Royce's imminent collapse had already reached the City and Fleet Street, and Nightingale Road was besieged by the world's media.

The entire town of Derby was stunned by the news of Rolls-Royce's collapse. The mood at Nightingale Road was indescribable. Personnel who had long worked at Nightingale Road found themselves either redundant or facing redundancy. An air of bereavement hung over Nightingale Road and Derby. Within the ranks of Rolls-Royce there had been rumours and counter rumours that the company had been experiencing serious financial problems regarding the RB211 project, and that some redundancies were to be expected, but no one actually thought that the company might go out of business. Likened to a national institution, Rolls-Royce was considered an intrinsic part of Great Britain, and the fall of Rolls-Royce was akin to the fall of the country or the monarchy. For senior Rolls-Royce managers the events of 4 February caused severe anguish, and reports at the time record general manager Geoffrey Fawn and personnel manager Dennis Hurd arriving to meet the workforce in a state of some distress.

Rolls-Royce won the contract to supply engines for Boeing's 757 airliner. The engine developed was the RB211-535 which provided 37,400lbs thrust. A Boeing 757 is pictured here in Air Europe livery, illustrating the point that the 535C engine, along with all the other RB211 variants, has proved to be among the most successful and fuel-efficient aero-engines available. (Courtesy Sir Henry Royce Memorial Foundation)

There were many stories of human tragedies: employees with 20 and 30 years' service were made redundant, and men were seen leaving the factory gates with tears in their eyes. Much of Derby had invested in Rolls-Royce, residents and businesses included, and many of them risked losing considerable sums of money. The Derbyshire Building Society was particularly vulnerable and small investors flocked to the society's office in Iron Gate. Queues of people stretched into the Market Place, and on one day alone £500,000 savings were withdrawn.

Philip Whitehead was the Labour Member of Parliament for Derby North at the time of the Rolls-Royce crash and he recalled the events of the morning of 4 February very clearly. The news arrived just as his youngest son was being born. 'We're bust' was the message. 'The news will be broadcast in an hour's time'.

In a number of respects E. Rupert Nicholson's appointment came as some relief to those associated with Rolls-Royce. Employees and unions staged demonstrations in Derby to save local jobs, and when trains were hired to take Rolls-Royce workers to London the protest group was given a police escort.

Under Rupert Nicholson's guidance the day-to-day running of Rolls-Royce was resumed, although on the first day of receivership the gates of Nightingale Road had remained firmly locked and all deliveries were turned away. When he met the workforce at Nightingale Road, Nicholson was expecting a rough ride, especially from union representatives. Certainly he met with some resentment, but overall Nicholson was greeted with cordiality and respect, and in the tradition of industrial relations at Rolls-Royce, he was given every assistance. From the outset it was clear to everybody that the receiver had not been appointed to wind down the company, but rather to promote it. The government was naturally anxious that military supplies were not affected, which at least gave some encouragement. Alas, not all government officials appreciated just how important the RB211 project was to the British aero industry, nor did they fully realise how imperative it was that Britain, and Rolls-Royce in particular, break into the market which until then had been dominated by the Americans. The main dissenting voice within the government was that, ironically, of Frederick Corfield, Minister of Aviation Supply.

Following his appointment, Rupert Nicholson did everything he could to secure the RB211's future. Three independent business specialists were chosen by the government to prepare a report on the engine's viability, and that document, compiled by Sir William Cook, Sir St John Elstub and Professor Holder, showed the project to be technically buoyant. The result was that the British government negotiated a new contract with Lockheed in May 1971, and later during that month Rolls-Royce (1971) Ltd, the new company, signed it in

With the advent of a new generation of jet airliners, Rolls-Royce was committed to designing an aero-engine to compete with America's engine-makers Pratt & Whitney and General Electric. RB211 development costs spiralled out of control, and spelled disaster for Rolls-Royce. On 4 February 1971 the company went into receivership, whereupon there began a sustained drive to rescue the firm and the livelihoods of the thousands of people affected by Rolls-Royce's collapse, in addition to those company employees who risked losing their jobs. This photograph shows the mood of angry Rolls-Royce workers who travelled to London to demonstrate for government backing and saving the company. There was a lot at stake, the future of Britain's aero-engine industry, the national economy and that of Derby and the surrounding area. (Courtesy Derby Evening Telegraph)

respect of supplying engines to the airframe manufacturer at a higher price than that originally negotiated. On 10 May an announcement was made to the effect that on 22 May all Rolls-Royce's assets would be transferred from the receiver to the government, and thereafter business at Nightingale Road would operate under the new name. The following day the route was set to produce the RB211; the old company of Rolls-Royce Limited went into liquidation on 4 October 1971. Government intervention meant nationalisation of Rolls-Royce, but it did at least revive the company's fortunes. It took 13 years for the company to get out of the red and into the black, and a further three years before it was re-privatised.

Rolls-Royce's collapse had a devastating effect on all aspects of the company, including the motor car division at Crewe. It is important to stress that at no time during the crisis was the motor car division bankrupt. In fact that part of Rolls-Royce remained financially independent and profitable, and it was for that reason among others that the chassis division was separated from the aero-engine concern and formed as a new company, Rolls-Royce Motors. On its formation Rolls-Royce Motors Ltd took over the assets of the motor car division and the oil-engine division, the latter being known as the diesel division. Rolls-Royce Motors remained in the hands of the receiver before being floated on the Stock Exchange as a separate entity.

With the formation of Rolls-Royce (1971) Ltd every effort was made to finalise the development of the RB211. While many senior personnel had been made redundant there was, nevertheless, the need to pool as much expertise as possible. Sir Stanley Hooker, who had retired in 1970, and whose ambition to become technical director of Rolls-Royce had failed to materialise, was recalled, along with fellow stalwarts Arthur Rubbra, Cyril Lovesey and Fred Morley. It was their combined efforts that turned the RB211 project into a successful reality. When the Lockheed TriStar went into operation during 1972 the RB211 performed more efficiently than could have been predicted.

It is an indication of Rolls-Royce's position as a world company that the government of the day moved quickly to save it, and in so doing secured tens of thousands of jobs worldwide. The high regard and reputation of Rolls-Royce was also at stake: as an international supplier of defence systems the demise of the company was untenable.

On 5 October Sir Kenneth Keith (later to become Lord Keith) was appointed

When Rolls-Royce employees and union officials arrived in London to demonstrate in order to persuade the government to support the company, thereby saving jobs in Derby in addition to those throughout the aviation and connected industries, they were met by a police escort, something unheard of at the time. Fighting for the RB211 and Rolls-Royce was akin to protecting Britain's most valuable asset. When news broke of Rolls-Royce's collapse it was not only company officials and employees that were stunned. The nation as a whole was horrified that a company associated with the Battle of Britain and the advent of the jet engine could be allowed to fall into obscurity. *(Courtesy Derby Evening Telegraph)*

chairman of Rolls-Royce. Keith, who had been deputy chairman of British European Airways since 1965, was well-versed in aviation matters, and throughout the 1970s proved to be a high-profile ambassador for the company. He was instrumental in achieving an impressive sales record which enabled Rolls-Royce to go from strength to strength.

Since going into service with the TriStar, applications of the RB211 have been seen on the Boeing 747 Jumbo Jet, Boeing 757 short to medium range airliner and numerous other airliners. The engine has been used industrially for a variety of applications including North Sea oil exploration.

A New Era: Better Times?

The mid to late 1970s should have been good years for Rolls-Royce. With the troublesome 1960s behind them, the 1,000th RB211 was built in 1980, and the company was at the leading edge of big engine technology. There were, nevertheless, quite serious problems: profits were not as high as had been anticipated owing to adverse exchange rates and high inflation, and losses of £22 million were recorded in 1976. A substantially greater loss of £58 million was recorded in 1979, which was attributed to a devastating industrial dispute. There was also serious overmanning, the company employing 62,000 people in 1980, 2,000 fewer than there had been in 1971. It was in 1980 that Francis McFadzean superseded Sir Kenneth Keith, and it was among the new chairman's duties to reduce Rolls-Royce's costs. This was achieved in two ways, by streamlining the company's operations so that much in-house manufacturing of smaller components was sub-contracted externally, and by reducing the workforce. The former measure created a number of redundancies, and additionally some 12,000 jobs were lost between 1981 and 1982, decreasing the workforce to some 46,000.

The economic downturn during the early 1980s brought more bad news to

Nightingale Road. Orders for new aircraft diminished and in 1982 sales were down by more than two-thirds compared with those of 1978/9. Rolls-Royce was not the only aero-engine manufacturer to feel the financial chill: Pratt & Whitney, together with General Electric, was keen to collaborate, and while Rolls-Royce travelled this route to some extent, it also sought partnerships elsewhere. The result was a combining of efforts on behalf of five countries, Britain, Germany, Italy, Japan and the US, to produce the V-2500 engine intended to power the Airbus A320 twin-engined airliner.

Ultimately Rolls-Royce did choose collaboration with an American manufacturer and signed an agreement with General Electric in 1984 to build the CF6-80C2 high bypass turbofan at Nightingale Road. Rolls-Royce was contracted to build 400 CF6s between 1984 and 1994, and the first was delivered in July 1986. The collaboration between the two companies became stressed when General Electric and Rolls-Royce both competed for a potential contract to supply engines to British Airways for its new fleet of Boeing 747 jets. Had Rolls-Royce won the contract all engines would have been built at Nightingale Road; if the contract were awarded to General Electric, the American manufacturer proposed that no more than a third of the engines would be built in Britain at Derby. The gulf between the two companies widened to the point that the relationship became untenable, and the arrangement ceased.

Economic recession during the mid-1980s took a further toll on the company's resources; at the end of 1984 the number of employees was reduced to 41,000, while trading figures for the years 1981–1983 showed a staggering loss of £191 million.

Rolls-Royce has been keenly involved in the military sector as well as commercial aviation. Successes in recent years have been seen in respect of the RB199 engine, as used with the Tornado fighter. Nowhere have Rolls-Royce engines been put to more spectacular use than in the British Aerospace Hawk trainers, which form the select and famous Red Arrows aerobatic team. Powered by Adour turbofans, the Red Arrows' Hawks thrill countless spectators every year at air shows up and down the country. Around the world Rolls-Royce Viper engines have been chosen by no fewer than 29 air forces to power such machines as the HJT-16 Kiran, Macchi MB-339 trainer and the ORAO twin-engined strike aircraft among others. Rolls-Royce engines were put to the test in 1982 when Harriers were so successful during the Falklands conflict, and again in 1991 when Tornados successfully completed their sorties during the Gulf War.

In recent years Rolls-Royce has formed a partnership with BMW, the culmination of several years of cooperation between the two companies. BMW began building aero-engines in 1916–17, and after 1954 such operations emerged as BMW Power Plant Production Co. Ltd to produce, among other equipment, Rolls-Royce Tyne engines under licence. The arrangement was eventually abandoned in favour of reconstructing the firm, and in 1990 a new company, BMW Rolls-Royce Aero-engines, was formed mainly to develop the B700, a new generation aero-engine that would supersede the Rolls-Royce Tay engines for commercial aircraft. The infrastructure of the partnership at the time of its establishment was impressive: BMW AG Munich had 66,000

Rolls-Royce Derby today. Rolls-Royce is as much a part of Derby's heritage as the railway works. The name and monogram rightly mark a quality and excellence that is appreciated the world over. (Courtesy Derby Evening Telegraph)

employees and a business turnover of 26 billion DM, and Rolls-Royce plc had 64,000 employees and a business turnover of £3 billion.

The 1990s proved to be good years for Rolls-Royce once the company had survived a general turndown in business that had affected world aviation. Oil prices rose substantially between 1990 and 1991, and following the Gulf War there was a major global recession. In 1995 the company acquired the American Allison Engine Company, and the following year Derby celebrated the news that Rolls-Royce had won an order to supply Malaysian Airlines with Trent 800 engines for its fleet of 17 new Boeing 777 airliners. The announcement of the contract was well received in Derby, especially as it assured employment for the Rolls-Royce workforce, then reported to number 10,000. In 1997 there was further good news for Derby when Delta and American Airlines chose the Trent 800 for their Boeing 777s, and in 1998 Rolls-Royce secured other substantial orders for its aero-engines.

Also in 1998 the Australian carrier Qantas elected to buy the RB211-524G/H-T engine for its fleet of Boeing 747-400s, while British Airways opted for the Trent 800 for its 32 Boeing 777s. British Airways also selected the V2500 engine in an order worth $2.5 billion, while Emirates became the first airline to power its entire fleet of aircraft with Trents.

11 September – In the Wake of Terrorism
In 2001 there was a further to boost to Derby when the British government announced it was injecting Rolls-Royce with £250 million to enable the

company to safeguard the jobs of 7,000 workers at Nightingale Road and provide for future development. The aero industry is a good barometer of economic performance. When times are financially good the aero industry responds favourably, and when there is a downturn it is aviation that is among the first to feel the iciness of recession. Throughout the 1990s Nightingale Road experienced both highs and lows, but the scenes at the factory gates were nothing as severe and demoralising as in the wake of the terrorist attacks in America during the autumn of 2001.

The events of 11 September had profound consequences for the world aviation industry, and problems regarding over capacity that had been simmering under the surface for many months were suddenly thrust to boiling point. To use a worn-out phrase, the industry was in meltdown.

Before the tragic events in America most long distance and transatlantic flights were operating on something of a knife-edge. In essence there were too many seats and too few passengers. When passengers stayed away in the aftermath of terrorism the cracks in the airline business opened wide. Swissair was one of the first casualties; Sabena, Belgium's national airline, another. Some operators grounded fleets while others, including British Airways and a number of American carriers, recorded huge losses and speculated that drastic cutbacks in manning levels would be effected within weeks and months. The numbers of airline and associated employees affected by the downturn in airline business around the world was staggering: in total early predictions forecast the loss of some 118,000 jobs. Fewer passengers meant fewer flights and the need for fewer aeroplanes; when orders for new aircraft were delayed or cancelled it was the aero-engine and other component manufacturers that were affected.

A month after the disasters in New York and Washington Rolls-Royce reported a disastrous downturn in business that led to the company announcing wholesale redundancies. Not only was this was bad news for Rolls-Royce workers and shareholders, it was a catastrophe for the many supporting component industries both within Derbyshire and nationally. Not for the first time in Rolls-Royce's history the city of Derby was besieged by an atmosphere of gloomy despondency.

On Friday 19 October the *Derby Evening Telegraph* carried the awesome headline against a backdrop of the statue of Sir Henry Royce 'Thousands of Rolls-Royce Jobs Axed'. Earlier that day Rolls-Royce had announced that 3,800 staff were to lose their jobs, 1,900 of them at Nightingale Road, along with some 1,000 contract employees. In all, 5,000 jobs would be lost worldwide in a move that would save the company around £250 million a year. The action, according to company senior executives, was necessary in order to resize overheads and realign cost and capacity with demand.

A statement issued by Rolls-Royce on Friday 19 October revealed that the company's civil aerospace business in 2002 could be expected to be 30 per cent lower than in 2001, notwithstanding the view that the firm's defence, marine and energy operations, which accounts for half its business, would remain unaffected. In the long term, the company's view is that business will recover, but not before 2003, and because the company has a young and growing installed base of engines which addresses all of the major civil aerospace sectors, it will generate increasing levels of aftermarket revenue.

Throughout the history of Rolls-Royce there have been periods of expansion and growth which have had positive effects on the morale of the workforce as well as providing increased prosperity to the city of Derby. There have also been times of deep depression when there has been no alternative other than to lay off workers. Apart from 1971 and the uncertainties surrounding the collapse of the company, no other event has had the same impact as the sudden downturn in business following terrorist attacks in America on 11 September 2001. This is the scene at Nightingale Road on 19 October 2001, following an announcement that huge job losses were imminent. (Courtesy Derby Evening Telegraph)

Union reaction to Rolls-Royce's announcement of the cutback in jobs was one of anger, especially as the company had informed the London Stock Exchange before telling the unions and personnel. Unlike in 1971 when Rolls-Royce employees heard of the company's plight over the works' tannoy system, workers were ushered into impromptu meetings throughout the factory to be told of forthcoming redundancies. Rolls-Royce management had, since August 2000, been implementing a policy to improve its competitiveness, something that would have resulted in the trimming of the workforce, and had been ongoing in order to save £159 million over a three-year period. Throughout its restructuring campaign Rolls-Royce had been careful not to divulge details of specific reductions in workforce numbers, an issue which had been the cause of some concern to both union leaders and company employees.

The decision to shed jobs at Derby was made at the company's monthly board meeting, which was held in London on Thursday 18 October. At that meeting the board was told that following the 11 September outrage Rolls-Royce's civil aerospace sales in 2002 were predicted to be £1 billion lower than anticipated, and that profitability would be halved.

Since the terrorist attacks of 11 September there had been concerns for the future within the Nightingale Road workforce of some 12,500. Morale was understandably low, and with every new rumour and ominous political prediction, it ebbed to even greater depths. Within days of the events in America both Boeing and Airbus announced that orders had been either deferred or cancelled, thus severely reducing demands for engines and associated components. With the grounding of aircraft because of the sudden and huge decline in the numbers of passengers, market stability was undermined as numerous airlines reviewed their operational strategies. All this resulted in a major fall in the value of Rolls-Royce shares from around 225 pence per share to around 133 pence per share, thus wiping off something like £1.5 billion off the value of the company on the London Stock Exchange.

Following the decision to axe jobs at Derby and at other sites around the country, union officials met with senior Rolls-Royce executives at Nightingale Road at 7am on 19 October to discuss the situation. Representing Rolls-Royce was chief executive John Rose, who was supported by his chief operating officer and president of Rolls-Royce civil aviation John Cheffins, and director of human resources John Rivers. In reviewing company policy in the context of the crisis John Cheffins was unable to rule out compulsory redundancies, and could only promise to reassess the situation once the result of voluntary severance programmes had been considered.

Job-loss announcements came as little surprise to the people of Derby, who had been anticipating such news for at least a week. Fears of cutbacks had been expressed in the *Derby Evening Telegraph* several days previously amid rumours circulating within Nightingale Road. Local politicians were quick to respond to the crisis and attempted to reduce workers' and Derby residents' fears for the future. In so doing they nevertheless had to remain mindful of the boost to the local economy that Rolls-Royce had directly and indirectly provided for a period in excess of 90 years.

Senior executives at Nightingale Road battled to highlight even the tiniest thread of good news among the demoralising events surrounding the decision to cut jobs. The fact that Rolls-Royce's market share of the aviation and aero-engine industries had grown from 10 per cent to 30 per cent in as many years came as little consolation to those whose jobs were affected. The overall position, while dire, was viewed with a degree of optimism, and John Cheffins went to lengths to assure Rolls-Royce personnel and the Derby community that the company was in a strong position to go forward.

As had been the case in 1971 over the financial collapse of Rolls-Royce, there were personal tragedies connected with the events of autumn 2001. The effects have been felt by those Rolls-Royce employees with many years service with the company, as well as by those starting out on their careers. A number of supporting industries, manufacturing and otherwise, were also in some way affected by the downturn in business and substantial job losses. It is anticipated that the original figures given by Rolls-Royce will, in the fullness of time, increase Derby-wide to some 9,000 or more positions.

In centring on the effects of the downturn in the aviation business it is important, nevertheless, not to lose sight of Derby's general economy. While Rolls-Royce is a major employer within the city and its environs, in truth the company has less of an influence on the area's prosperity and resources than it had in the 1980s and 1990s, and considerably less than in the 1970s. Opinion from inside the city's business community suggests that the events of September 2001 had a lesser effect than the financial collapse of Rolls-Royce in 1971. A survey undertaken by Derby's Chamber of Commerce indicated that 70 per cent of its members believed that they would remain unaffected by the

The picture says it all. Having been told that more than 2,000 jobs were to be axed because of the downturn in demand for aero-engines following the events in America of 11 September 2001, Rolls-Royce workers at Derby face an uncertain future. History has shown that even for a company as resourceful as Rolls-Royce, existence can be extremely tenuous. It is not only Rolls-Royce jobs that are in jeopardy, but also hundreds, possibly thousands more in industries and businesses associated with aviation both at Derby, in the surrounding area, and countrywide. (Courtesy Derby Evening Telegraph)

downturn in the avionics industry and Rolls-Royce's aero-engine business in particular, mainly owing to the fact that Derby's economy had diversified during recent years.

The consensus of opinion within Derby's business community was that the job losses announced at Rolls-Royce could be absorbed into alternative industries, especially as there is a shortage of skills in the area. As soon as job cutbacks were publicised, the city's Chamber of Commerce put into action a campaign to help those people facing redundancy; action groups and surgeries were established in order that skills could be deployed in various ways, provision made for re-training, and assistance offered in finding alternative employment.

Historically Rolls-Royce, along with British Rail Engineering, has had a major influence on Derby as an industrial engineering base. Today, Derby is recognised as a centre of excellence in terms of engineering, the quality and skills employed at Rolls-Royce having had a considerable authority throughout the company's tenure in the city. The high degree of training imparted by Rolls-Royce has been passed on to other organisations, and as a result many smaller businesses have benefited.

Despite the positive mood of the city's business quarter, there is, nevertheless, a degree of concern that is shared by the wider community. In the short term it is the consumable industries and businesses that will suffer, such as tourism and leisure, restaurants, the property market and providers of luxury goods. British manufacturing industries have, throughout the post-war years, undergone a dramatic transformation, and predictions confirm that this will continue. In its place there has been a generation of alternative skills that encompass telecommunications and financial services, and within the Derbyshire area there has been a proliferation of call centres and similar establishments.

Overall, Rolls-Royce employed 43,500 people worldwide before 11 September; and in the short term envisaged reducing that number by 5,000, 3,800 in the United Kingdom across its sites, and 1,200 overseas. What will happen to Rolls-Royce in the long term is a matter of conjecture. The company is the world-leading aero-engine manufacturer; it employs a highly skilled workforce, and whatever happens in the immediate future there will remain a demand for air travel and new aircraft.

Within the foreseeable future the search for alternative fuels will lead to the design of revolutionary aeroplanes. Just as the jet engine pioneered a new dimension in aviation technology in the immediate post-war years, and Concorde introduced supersonic air travel, so Rolls-Royce, in the shadow of the statue of Sir Henry, will be present to take aviation into a new era.

INDEX

ND - #0235 - 270225 - C0 - 260/195/8 - PB - 9781780914978 - Gloss Lamination